T H E   N E W
AUSTRIAN ARCHITECTURE

THE NEW
AUSTRIAN ARCHITECTURE

FRANK DIMSTER

Introduction by James Steele, Jr.

RIZZOLI
NEW YORK

For Dagmar

First published in the United States of America in 1995 by
Rizzoli International Publications, Inc.
300 Park Avenue South, New York, NY 10010

Copyright ©1995 Rizzoli International Publications, Inc.

Library of Congress Cataloging-in-Publication Data

Dimster, Frank.
    The new Austrian architecture / by Frank Dimster ; with an essay
by James Steele, Jr.
        p.   cm.
    ISBN 0–8478–1757–1. — ISBN 0–8478–1758–X (pbk.)
1. Architecture, Modern—20th century—Austria. 2. Architecture–
–Austria.   I. Steele, James, 1943–   .   II. Title.
NA1008.D56   1995   95–3185
720'.9436'09048—dc20   CIP

Designer: Abigail Sturges

Printed and bound in Singapore

*Jacket photograph: Gustav Peichl, Städel Museum, Frankfurt,
Germany, 1990*
*Jacket drawing: Adolf Krischanitz, perspective, Traisen Pavilion,
St. Pölten, 1988*
Frontispiece: Gustav Peichl, ORF Broadcasting Studios, Vienna, 1983
*Back cover (hardcover only): Szyszkowitz-Kowalski, Institute for
Biochemistry and Biotechnology, Technical University of Graz, 1991*

Illustration Credits
Numbers refer to page numbers.

© Abuja: 177
© Oskar Dariz: 180–81, 183
Martha Deltsios: 92–107
G. Domenig Archive: 47 (top)
© Driendl∗Steixner: 56–63, 65–67
© Foto Schwingenschlögl: 28 (model)
© Fotoatelier Gerlach: 27, 28 (top), 30 (bottom), 31, 33 (right)
© Damjan Gale: 176, 184, 188 (top)
© Helmut Heistinger: 175
Peter Hermann: 46
Bernard Hohengasser: 120–21
Atelier Hans Hollein: 76–77, 78, 80–81, 84–85, 88–90
Franz Hubmann: 30 (top)
Klaus Kada: 108–09, 112–13, 123
Karl Kofler: 44–45, 47 (bottom, both), 49
Nadine Krier: 124–25, 128–29, 132–33
Kühne: 28 (bottom), 29 (top)
Christof Lackner: 142–45
Luftreportagen Hausmann/Wien: 140
Faraidoon Mohiden: 213
© Ivan Nemec: 171, front cover
Monika Nikolic: 172–73
Paul Ott: 116–17
Josef Pausch © Ortner & Ortner: 156–57, 160–61
Gustav Peichl: 163–64, 170, frontispiece
Roland Rainer: 22, 24, 25, 26, 29 (bottom), 32, 33 (top)
Ali Schafler: 162, 167, 169, 218–19
Schiessl: 23, 33 (bottom left)
Hannes Schild: 149–50
© Spilluttini, Margherita: 68–73, 134–35, 138–39, 148, 152–55,
200–202, 216
© Rupert Steiner: 204–05, 208–09
Szyszkowitz-Kowalski: 210–12, 214–15, back cover
Elfi Tripamer: 51, 54–55
Willig, Hajo: 220–21, 224
© Gerald Zugmann: 37–43, 185, 188 (bottom), 189, 192–93,
195–97
Foto Zumtobel: 217

Acknowledgments

I wish to express my gratitude to Don M. Dimster for his extensive assistance in preparing this volume over a very long period of time. In addition, I would like to express my gratitude to the University of Southern California and to Dr. Christian Prosl, the Consul General of Austria in Los Angeles. Above all, I would like to thank the architects for their work and for their efforts to provide the material that is featured here.

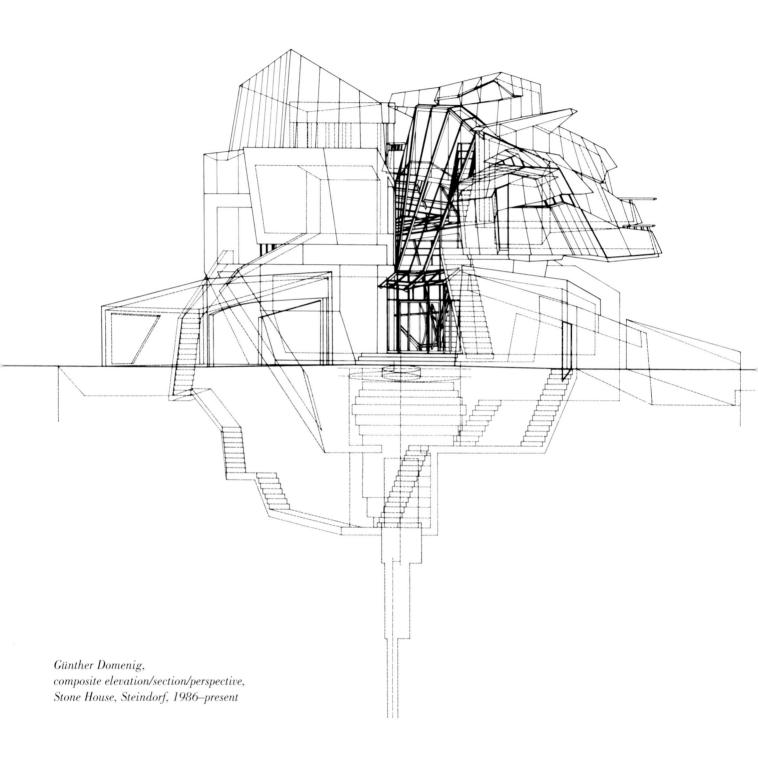

Günther Domenig,
composite elevation/section/perspective,
Stone House, Steindorf, 1986–present

Contents

Introduction

FIN DE SIÈCLE COMES FULL CIRCLE

James Steele, Jr.

Many who are aware of the current international architectural scene are not familiar with developments in Austria, and may sense that little has happened there recently beyond the activities of a few well-published superstars—and certainly nothing to rival the frenetic, brilliant period prior to World War I. The wide-ranging presentation here does much to dispel this attitude, and reveals many different agenda and directions that in their own way are comparable to the rich complexity of Vienna at the turn of the century. The city was then and still is the heart, soul, and primary site of Austria's architectural diversity.

A Distinguished Legacy

Any review of historical influences should begin with Otto Wagner. He is undeniably the dominant figure in Austrian architectural history, not only because of the sheer number of his commissions but also because of his recognition of the changes that industrialization made possible, his willingness to embrace and champion those changes late in his career, and his wide influence throughout central and eastern Europe.

Wagner began his career by following older classicists like Josef Kornhäusel, Heinrich von Ferstel, and Theophilus Hansen, as evident in his scheme for the Länderbank of 1883–84 (left). But the degree of invention that project reveals, in its use of a central rotunda to reconcile two different axes of the site, already indicates a higher level of ingenuity at work. The Länderbank also incorporates historical references to San Vitale in Ravenna and Fischer von Erlach's early-eighteenth-century Karlskirche in Vienna. Wagner continued to establish his reputation with the construction of the First Villa Wagner in Vienna in 1886 and by entering several important competitions outside Vienna. His Hoyos House of 1891 brought official recognition, and his appointment as a professor at the Academy of Fine Arts in 1894 provided academic credibility.

Wagner's appointment in 1894 as the supervising architect of Vienna's Stadtbahn, or Municipal Railway, further confirmed his new stature. He was prescient in realizing that the city's first mass-transit system would be more than the sum of its parts: the stations would constitute a new aspect of the public domain, one by which people would continue to identify their city, and themselves as part of it. Wagner expanded a system of entrance canopies and lighting standards inspired by the Paris Metro to give each Vienna station its own identity. In these works and others, such as his bridges and locks for the Danube Canal, Wagner exhibited a broad civic vision shared by his contemporary, Camillo Sitte.

The two architects had different approaches, however. As Franco Borsi has described: "When Camillo Sitte and Otto Wagner launched their attacks on the world of the Ringstrasse, the former was looking to the past while the latter was looking into the future. Both rebelled against the dense grid layout of modern cities, the alienating monumental scale of the buildings, the widely favored broad arterial roads. However, Sitte invoked a model drawn from the medieval city as a free-form cluster, while Wagner repudiated historicism and championed a new rationality with its roots in modern life."[1]

Wagner promoted his own version of that rationality in his book *Moderne Architektur* (1895), which addressed new building materials and the impact of an expanding urban scale caused by rural migration to the cities. Wagner's own style changed dramatically during this period in terms of the materials he used and how he applied them. In two of his major commissions from 1902 to 1907, the Steinhof Church and the Postal Savings Bank, the ponderous use of stone in his earlier work was replaced by thin cladding attached to an inner frame by exposed bronze bolts, giving the surface a mechanized, riveted appearance. Wagner introduced new materials such as aluminum, used in pencil-thin columns and canopies, which emphasized the new attention to surface and lightness in his work. At the Steinhof Church, this attention resulted in a discrepancy between the interior and exterior appearance of the dome, showing the degree to which Wagner had begun to break with tradition. This attitude toward thinness and layering finally reached its synthesis in Wagner's masterpiece, the Postal Savings Bank.

To the Age, Its Art

Wagner, the epitome of an establishment architect, created a scandal in 1899 by joining the secessionist Austrian

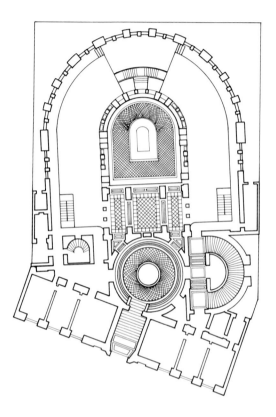

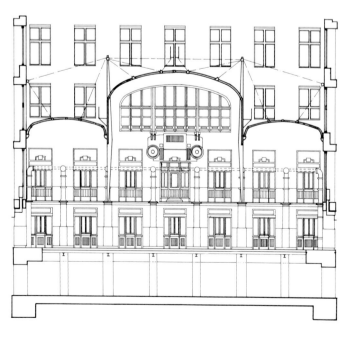

Association of Artists founded two years earlier and led by Gustav Klimt. Beyond its well-known exhibitions and its headquarters building in Vienna designed by Joseph Maria Olbrich in 1898, the Secession was extremely important for promoting trade skills. In 1899 one of its charter members, Felician von Myrbach, became director of the School of Arts and Crafts and hired Secessionists Josef Hoffmann and Koloman Moser as professors. These events were significant given the School's wide-ranging influence; as Ezio Godoli explains, "Within the Hapsburg's system of art and trade education, the schools of arts and crafts . . . were at the apex of a pyramid based on one hundred-and-fifty trade schools located throughout the Empire. . . . [Among these] the Vienna School of Arts and Crafts held a position of cultural primacy. Many teachers trained there later worked in trade schools throughout the Empire. . . . They helped to spread 'Viennese taste' throughout the whole German-speaking world."[2]

In 1903 Moser and Hoffmann established the Wiener Werkstätte as the Austrian counterpart of William Morris's Arts and Crafts Movement in England. Based on a similar philosophical resistance to mass production, the Wiener Werkstätte worked in close collaboration with and was an outlet for the School of Arts and Crafts. By all accounts Hoffmann's output was staggering, as if a river of objects had suddenly come pouring through the dam of tradition broken by Wagner. Frequently an entire tea service in silver was sketched on a single sheet of paper, each piece stamped with a "datum" or identification number to mark its sequence in production. As with Morris's workshop, production included textiles, glassware, furniture, silverware, jewelry, lamps, wall coverings, hardware, and anything else that fell into the purview of *Gesamtkunstwerk*, the total work of art that would transform those who participated in its use.

This integral approach, of course, meant a costly commitment for most clients, so when Hoffmann met Adolphe Stoclet, who had the means to finance such production, he was delighted to focus the multiple talents of the Wiener Werkstätte on a single project, the Stoclet House in Brussels, of 1905–11. As with Wagner's Postal Savings Bank and the Michaelerplatz Building by Adolf Loos, the Stoclet House stands out as Hoffmann's own tour de force. It combines the severe lines of the Purkersdorf

Sanitarium, built one year earlier, with heightened luxury afforded by an unrestricted budget. Marble panels joined at corners by gilded seams, rather than the exposed bronze bolts favored by Wagner, give both exterior and interior a strangely superficial quality. The dining room mosaics by Gustav Klimt, executed on marble panels that clad the entire room, remain one of the most irrefutable examples of the true integration between art and architecture that initially characterized the Wiener Werkstätte. This ideal was irrevocably lost when Klimt and several other founding members left the Secession in 1905 to work on their own.

Another protagonist on this supercharged artistic landscape was Joseph Maria Olbrich, whose name is usually associated only with his Secession Building but who contributed far more given his singular affinity with the wider art nouveau network across Europe. Olbrich entered the State School of Applied Arts in Vienna in 1883, when Camillo Sitte became its director, and transferred to the Special School for Architecture at the Academy of Fine Arts in 1890. His final project at the Academy won the Rome Prize in 1893 and attracted the attention of Otto Wagner, who offered Olbrich a job in his office. He worked there before leaving for Italy and again when he returned six months later.

Early in 1897 partisans in the Interior Ministry arranged for a site near the Ringstrasse for a new Secession exhibition building; Olbrich was chosen to design it. The turbulent progress of the building's design matched the rebellious intentions of the Secession group itself. Initial sketches were far less restrained than the eventually realized design, exhibiting more of the curvilinear outline that has come to represent Olbrich's style. In ardent written descriptions of the project's evolution the architect speaks subjectively of "frozen feelings," but as finally completed the Secession Building is somber. It would have been more so had the elevations approved by Secession leader Klimt been implemented, since these did not include the dome of entwined laurel leaves, once plated with gold, that has come to symbolize the movement. Not even the dome, however, deflected general public disdain for the building or prevented it from being nicknamed "The Golden Cabbage."

In spite of mixed reviews the Secession Building drew attention to Olbrich, and in the commissions that followed he began to be more expansive, to give free reign to his exuberance. Many of Olbrich's private houses, such as the Bahr House, recall the steeply pitched roofs and rustic materials of the vernacular architecture of his native Silesia, with a dominant dendritic, curvilinear outline. The Secession Building brought him to the attention of Ernst Ludwig, Grand Duke of Hesse, who was establishing an artists colony in Darmstadt and invited Olbrich to participate. Olbrich went to Darmstadt for the first time in 1899, the year that the *Dokument Deutscher Kunst* (Document of German Art) exhibit was first announced. As the only architect in the original Darmstadt group, Olbrich was naturally chosen to design the main studio building, named the Ernst Ludwig House after the patron of the new community. Directly opposite, Olbrich designed a house for himself; eventually he went on to execute many other buildings in the colony, based mainly on Teutonic vernacular models. His Wedding Tower and Exhibition Building, built in commemoration of Ludwig's marriage to Princess Eleonore in 1905, remains a focal point of the Darmstadt colony.

Adolf Loos: The Other

Olbrich has been credited with attempting to transform Vienna into a "New Byzantium" through his use of sensual line and color, but Adolf Loos used the more theoretical approach of writing and teaching.[3] As Godoli has noted in discussing the Wagner School: "In their iconography, Wagner's students reclaimed and used freely many Oriental forms (mostly Byzantine and Islamic) and this took on a symbolic significance charged with esoteric allusions. The 'cosmic cupola' thus stood as a symbol for a whole range of philosophical creeds."[4]

For Loos this reclamation was more sophisticated, involving his perception of classical Greek architecture's generating force and its continuation through the Roman period. Loos sought to revive the Platonic injunction that equated *symmetria*, or commensurability, with beauty and extended into the search for pure geometric forms that might bring order and certainty to the chaos of human existence. This is evident in his reduction of the architectural equation to its most essential parts and in his *Raumplan*, or "plan of volumes"—the inevitable Platonic solids that give his work such clarity.

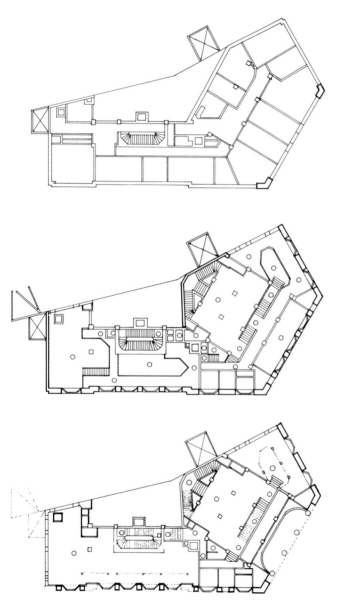

*Adolf Loos, Goldman &
Salatsch store, floor plans,
Vienna, 1910–1911.*

Loos frequently acknowledged his respect for Otto Wagner, yet a closer look shows that the two architects were diametrically different.[5] Wagner came from a wealthy family; in spite of his move toward the Secession in 1899 he had always been a model establishment architect, with political and academic connections that allowed him to build a great deal. Loos, on the other hand, was the son of a stone mason from Brno (then considered to be a suburb of Vienna) and was the archetypal polemicist. In his first three years in the capital city he produced articles such as "Die Potemkinsche Stadt," criticizing the "Potemkin village" character of the facades along the Ringstrasse that had been designed in part by Wagner and those he influenced.[6] Loos's facility with words proved to be a two-edged sword; it attracted notoriety but excluded him from the inner circle of influence that Wagner enjoyed. Loos's founding of the journal *Das Andere* is clear evidence of his hope that writing as well as building would promote the social awareness of design.

Loos's remarkable design of 1910 for the Goldman & Salatsch store on the Michaelerplatz in Vienna, one of his largest commissions, graphically exposes the differences between the two architects. The site, opposite the Hofburg, presented many difficulties; in addition to being surrounded by venerated buildings it had an irregular polygonal shape that precluded a symmetrical solution. Loos logically chose the facade facing the Michaelerplatz for the primary entrance and recessed it behind a row of columns, with delightful results. In one of the few comprehensive retrospectives of Loos's work, Ludwig Münz notes that "the facade of the Michaelerplatz was especially distinguished by making the lower two stories into a kind of lofty ground floor with mezzanine above. . . . Thanks to this colonnade of four unpieced columns, set well apart, the facade does not shut out the Michaelerplatz in a hard and rigid line, but allows it to extend a little way into the building. . . . "[7] This subtle spatial recognition of the square continues around the perimeter, which, as Münz says, "does not just turn the corner into the Kohlmarkt and the Herrengasse at obtuse angles but first accentuates the arrises by pulling them out, albeit almost imperceptibly. Thus the adjoining axes of the building in the Herrengasse become a kind of projection in front of the remaining wall. . . . The same principle was followed by Palladio in his

*Adolf Loos, Goldman &
Salatsch store, section and
proposed facade treatment,
Vienna, 1910–1911.*

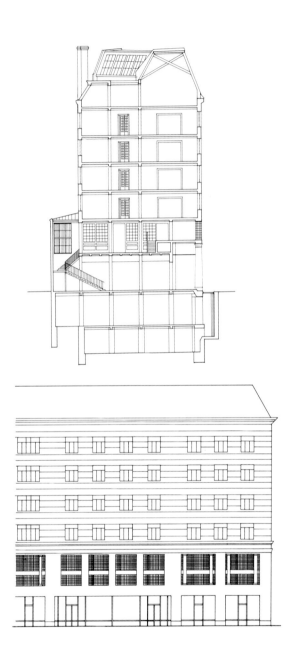

palaces at Vicenza. Unobtrusively, yet suggestively, the
whole frontage is stretched along the square—it even seems
to curve."[8] The considerate civic etiquette expressed on the
first two stories changes radically on the remainder of the
elevation, however. In contrast to the street level, with its
marble imported from Euboea, in Greece, the upper four
floors are rendered in plaster over brick, and the windows
simply punched into the wall with no decorative surround.

When the scaffolding was removed from the Goldman &
Salatsch building, public outcry was so intense that the
municipal authorities demanded changes, which Loos
refused to carry out. Such architectural severity was
considered heretical in Vienna in 1910, in a city grown
accustomed to the neoclassical ostentation of the Ring. The
strength of that neoclassical tradition and the subtle
Palladian variation that Münz identified in the
Michaelerplatz project is an important key to Loos's
contribution. Rather than destroy tradition, Loos's intention
was to refine it, to explore its spirit through an
epistemological process of formal layering and the
juxtaposition of materials, as opposed to mere surface
treatment.

In conjunction with this geometry, Loos's use of marble
imported from quarries as far away as Greece and Egypt
indicated his intentional foreshortening of history. The
unforgettable marble revetments of Justinian's most daring
experiments, such as the Hagia Sophia, and their echoes in
Ravenna are the philosophical if not spiritual precursors of
Loos's Kärntner Bar and villa interiors, just as the
fourteenth-century Christian mosaics in St. Savior in Chora
(Kariye Camii) in Istanbul prefigure Gustav Klimt's
mystical images. Beyond this inveterate, if admittedly
occluded historicity, however, is Loos's basic belief in the
Greek ideal of simplifying daily routine and the artifacts of
life to enhance the nobility of the mind.

The Spaces of Modern Life

Loos's *Raumplan*, which he felt could not be adequately
described in the flatness of a photograph, relied upon the
personal experience of three dimensions for its impact, with
the difference between the public exterior of a building and
the private interior clearly expressed. An axial wall was

Adolf Loos, Winternitz House,
elevations and sections,
Prague-Smichov, 1931–1932

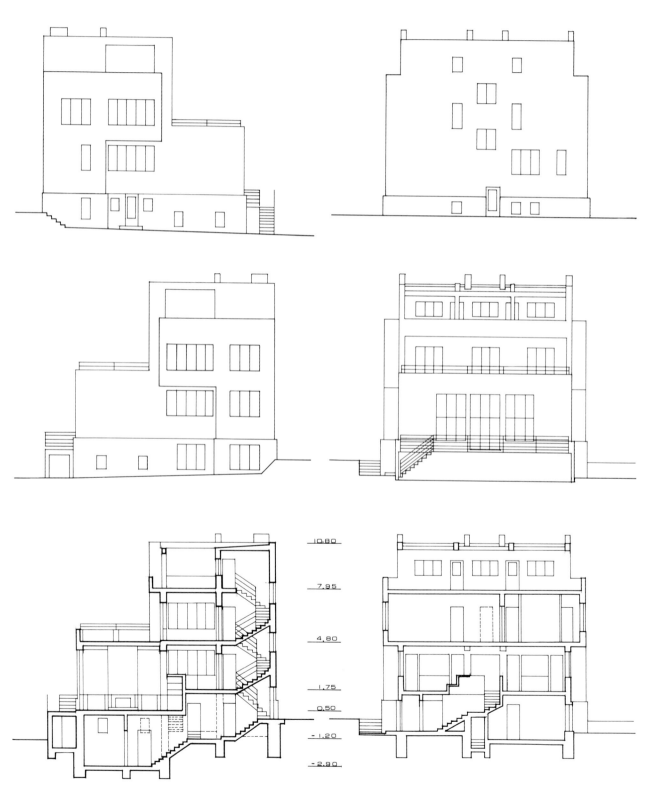

typically used as an ordering device to divide the volumes, and while not always symmetrically central it was clearly established as a bilateral division and generated other partitions and levels.[9]

This has particular bearing upon contemporary Austrian architecture. In a telling analysis, Beatriz Colomina has pointed out that Loos, in stubbornly adhering to this dichotomy between exterior and interior, was simply perpetuating a singularly Viennese trait of creating a mask to distinguish the formal from the informal or personal. As she says, "This Viennese attention to the mask finally focuses on the *inner* space. One might say that it is the mask that allows this space its content, that makes it 'intimate.'"[10] And, in determining the architect's realization of this, she says, "Loos had realized that modern life was proceeding on two irreconcilable levels, the one of our experience as individuals, *the other* of our existence as society; and that which we could understand as abstract minds, namely as a collectivity, we were already unable to live as individuals. . . . For Loos it was hopeless to try to render the outside in the experiential terms of the inside. They are two irreducible systems. The interior speaks the language of culture, the language of the experience of things; the exterior speaks the language of civilization, that of information."[11]

Loos lived to see Europe threatened by World War II, while Hoffmann died in 1956; but by the end of World War I, Wagner, Olbrich, Klimt, and Schiele were gone, as was the spirit of fin-de-siècle Vienna. The unlikely circumstances that coalesced to make the city's intellectual life a microcosm of Europe's at the end of the century are complex, but it is clear that such concentration of talent in many fields at one time and in one place has few historical counterparts.

In a thoughtful reflection on this era, Kirk Varnedoe, who directed the "Vienna 1900: Art, Architecture & Design" exhibition at the Museum of Modern Art in New York in 1986, observed that all too often there is a tendency among historians to attempt to read more consistency into this concentration than actually existed. As he says, "Many other cities, such as Berlin, Prague, or Munich, produced great writers, philosophers, and scientists and raised social issues of enormous consequences. Many of these cities also had important artists and active Secession movements. But

Vienna set itself apart by the eruption of talent in all the visual arts and by the particular Viennese sensibility, the *Lebensgefühl*, associated with those achievements." He goes on to caution, however, that "no matter how attractively we package our image of the 'gay apocalypse,' this discrepancy will not, and should not, be disguised. If we study the circumstances that united creators as diverse as Wittgenstein and Kraus and Loos and Altenberg and Musil, without discerning the differences in power and originality that separated them, then we miss something crucial."[12]

The Contemporary Expression of a Grand Tradition

The powerful memory of that apocalypse reverberates to the present day, and there is a tendency to compare the achievements of contemporary Austrian architects with those of their predecessors—to search for similarities and continuities, or to invent them if none exist. Each of the architects presented here, however, has a unique vision and a personal style that reflect both the fin-de-siècle legacy of individuality and the influence of recent masters such as Roland Rainer.

Since World War II, Rainer has sustained the greatest influence over aspiring and practicing architects in Austria. In the best tradition of Otto Wagner and Adolf Loos, he believes firmly in a questioning attitude and circumscribed change, offering an alternative to the popular, more traditional approach led by Clemens Holzmeister. Rainer's rational, user-oriented architecture is decidedly anti-historicist in its spare, non-symbolic use of form and clean surfaces. While he is not convinced of the classical legacy's enduring relevance, he adopts a social agenda similar to Loos's, expressed in housing schemes that have consistently posed alternatives to the single-family detached urban house. These include his early Veitingergasse (1953); Terraced Housing, Ternitz (1956); and most significantly, Puchenau Garden City just outside Linz (phases I and II, 1965–present). Here he freely implemented his ideas about segregating automobile and pedestrian traffic; the importance of orientation; the relationship between buildings and the environment; and an efficient, self-

*Hans Hollein, Haas Haus,
section, Vienna, 1990.*

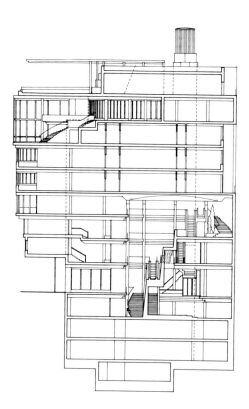

sustaining infrastructure. Rainer's ability to approach
problems objectively and at large scale, together with his
appreciation of regional imperatives, have deeply inspired
the current generation of Austrian architects reviewed here.

Precedents for Postmodernism

Rainer has noted that many contemporary Austrian
architects adopted postmodernism not out of conviction but
rather for the instant notoriety it often imparts. In the
current frenzy to label, categorize, exhibit, and annotate,
this might be misinterpreted in Hans Hollein's case. More
than any of his contemporaries, Hollein represents a
Hoffmannesque sensibility, and some attribute his flirtation
with postmodernism not to a desire for notoriety but to the
influence of a more substantial cultural tradition. As
Friedrich Achleitner has said, "To do justice to Hollein,
one cannot ignore the Viennese reality, where there is a
tradition that is too old and a sensibility that is too highly
developed with regard to the architectural setting as a
counter-reality or a substitute reality. Going right back to
the Baroque, and maybe even earlier, the ambivalence of
the media of music and architecture (arising out of the
repression of literature by the Hapsburgs) was favoured
above the presentation of evident realities, and came to
reflect collective and individual psychic states. . . . Vienna
possessed a tradition of aesthetic heightening of reality, a
long praxis of artificial remoteness. The techniques of
montage, collage, alienation, striking illusions and
disarming quotation are not cultivated in language alone."[13]
　Hollein's early, jewel-like exercises, such as the Retti
Candle Company in Vienna (1965), with its microscopic
focus on detail, materials, and production, underscore
Achleitner's point. Comparing these projects to Hollein's
monumental Haas Haus in Vienna and his contextual
design for the Salzburg Guggenheim Museum reveals an
architect slowly coming to terms with both his humanistic
heritage and large-scale commissions. These factors merge
in the controversial Haas Haus, where Hollein's response to
the stringent parameters of the curved corner site facing the
open spaces of the Stephansplatz and the Graben, and to
the contextual imperatives of the nearby cathedral, have
confirmed his skill as a designer and his familiarity with

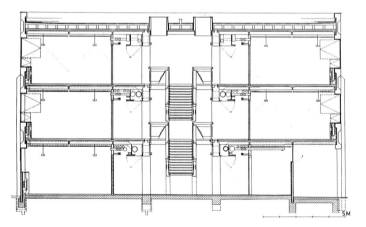

Cross section

Roman Catholic Church
1979–1980, Leonding

This extension of a baroque church is built between the
priest's quarters and the old cemetery. The main room, with
its eight corners, is based on the traditional early Christian
church plan. The main altar stands in the middle of the
room, where the floor is slightly depressed. Light penetrat-
ing through the skylight draws the eye from the altar
upward, appearing to lift it toward the sky. A gallery around
the perimeter of the octagon connects the new structure to
the existing church, the priest's private quarters, and the
main entrance facing the plaza. Spatial unity is achieved in
the spirit of the basilican temple.

THE
ARCHITECTS

COOP HIMMELBLAU

Ronacher Theater Complex ▪ Vienna ▪ 1987

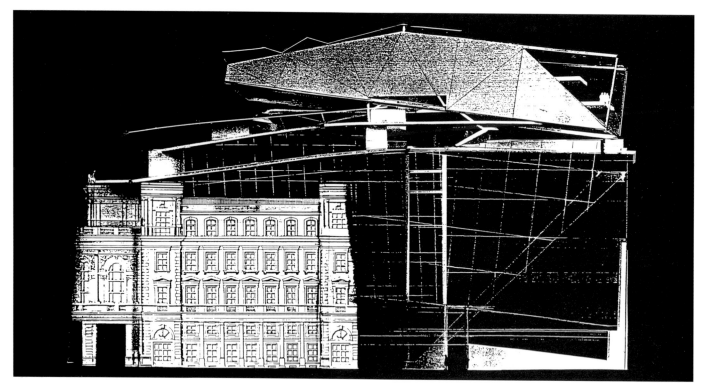

Coop Himmelblau, headed by Wolf D. Prix and Helmut Swiczinsky, has created a distinct and widely recognized aesthetic. They employ controversial and nonconformist strategies, such as drawing with their eyes closed, that would seem to meet resistance in a tradition-bound city like Vienna. However, that city has been host to some of Coop Himmelblau's most important work. The Ronacher Theater Complex uses the conflict between old and new to its advantage: while it is a remodeling of the existing Ronacher Theater, the project hails a new modern era by exploiting current developments in communications technology.

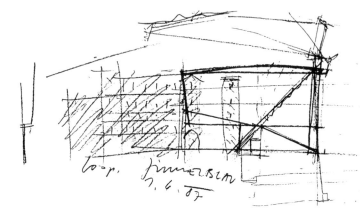

This project incorporates spaces for the public previously considered off-limits: rehearsal rooms, backstage areas, a roof terrace with an open-air stage, restaurants on the lower level and the roof, a public *videotheque*, and bars in the foyers. The one area not open to the public is the "black box," whose blank exterior walls screen an idealized interior and create the illusion of theater. This multimedia complex was planned to accommodate every form of performing art, with performances staged from the basement to the roof.

COOP HIMMELBLAU

Funder Factory 3 ▪ St. Veit/Glan, Carinthia ▪ 1988

This utilitarian building received the same dedication and philosophical approach as have all other Coop Himmelblau designs, as the architects sought to create an unmistakable identity for the factory. The project consists of two elements: the central area for producing energy and the production hall. A bridge running three meters above the main space connects the two.

The hall is constructed of steel, with precast concrete plates for the lower section of the walls. Above the concrete plates, metal panels complete the enclosure. The southwest corner, made of steel and glass, appears to have toppled over.

The central area for energy production is made of reinforced concrete. The wall system resembles that of the main hall. Three chimneys dance along the central part of the building, coming in partial contact with each other.

The connecting bridge approaches the roof of the central area and continues as a bent bridge construction. Half of the length of the bridge is covered with metal, and the other half with acrylic plates. The bridge cuts through the large folded roof, the building's fifth facade, which is visible from the main road.

Cross section

Isometric

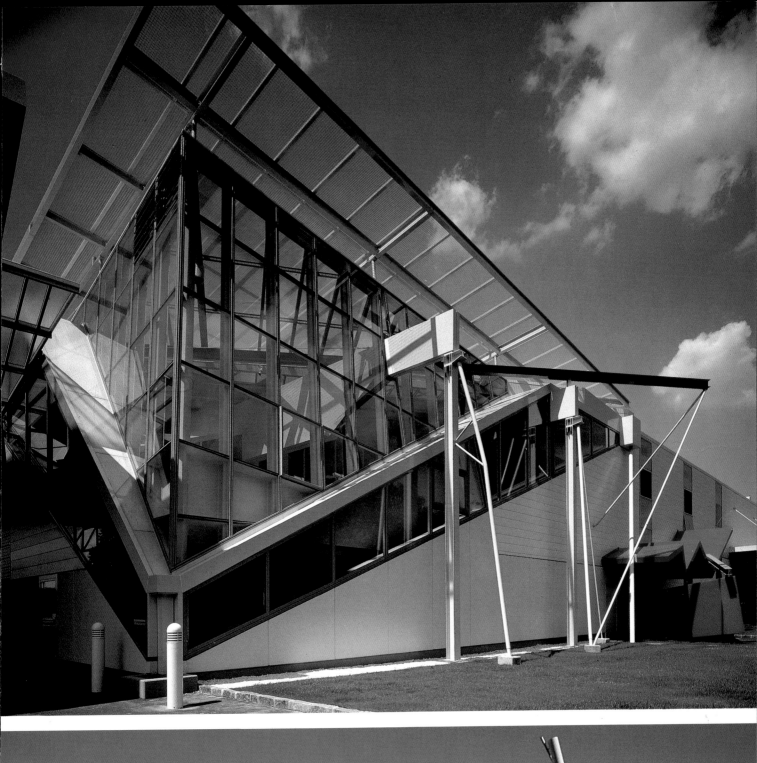

COOP HIMMELBLAU

Rooftop Remodeling, Falkestrasse 6 ▪ Vienna ▪ 1989

Floor plan

Coop Himmelblau's most famous project is this rooftop remodeling in Vienna, which was instrumental in liberating previous notions of how we conceive and execute architecture.

The preliminary design eschewed roof alcoves and turrets, turning its back on local proportions, materials, and colors. Instead, the architects visualized a line of energy starting at the street and spanning the project, breaking the existing roofline and opening it up. The image of an inverted lightning bolt arching over the roof guided the design process.

The taut arc is the steel backbone of the project. Tautness also describes tension; extremely tenuous connections between different steel members, with their apparent levity, juxtaposed against neatly articulated glass planes create tension in the resulting spaces. Steel beams metamorphose from representations of weight and immense load-bearing capabilities into light and lightness. The main lighting fixture over the conference table is a floating I-beam with recessed fixtures.

Section

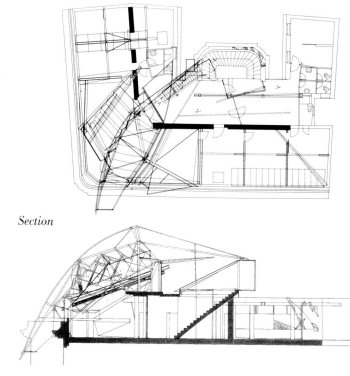

GÜNTHER DOMENIG

Branch Office, Zentralsparkasse ▪ *Vienna-Favoriten* ▪ *1979*

Günther Domenig believes that buildings must convey a sense of responsibility that extends beyond function and mere economy, in both materials and ideas. Building should be judged by a standard that encompasses a broader sense of purpose. Architecture is capable of transmitting a multitude of messages, including a feeling for the emotional context of events that transpired during the planning and building process. A building can express itself through a language that places it at a specific point in time. Domenig maintains that because of this deeper responsibility a bank branch must be more than an impressive, stable-looking establishment building where the usual financial transactions take place.

The Zentralsparkasse collects art for its walls, and this branch offers a place for public exhibitions about the Favoriten district of Vienna. Domenig adopted the contours and angles of the surrounding urban area and projected them onto the outer and inner form of the new construction. The mountainous roofscape toward the rear is constantly transfigured as one's vantage point changes. Once again unfamiliar geometric forms arise out of contextual lines and angles.

The functional layout of the interior is visible from without. Displaced half floors converge in a single room with a protruding snout that fuses exterior and interior space. Upper stories house community functions, a delineation accentuated by the segmented facade. Materials maintain their true forms. Both the structural framework and technical installations remain visible so that the function of each component is conspicuous and given a dynamic visual expression.

Similarly, the skin of the building transforms itself under the heat of the sun, the temporary buckling causing an accentuated melting effect as it twists and reflects light from its surface, recycling the contextual lines.

Ground floor plan   *Upper level plan*

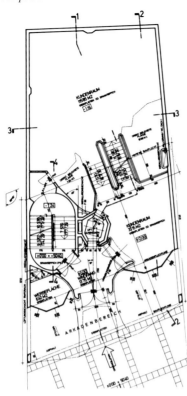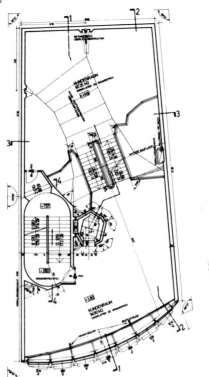

Sections

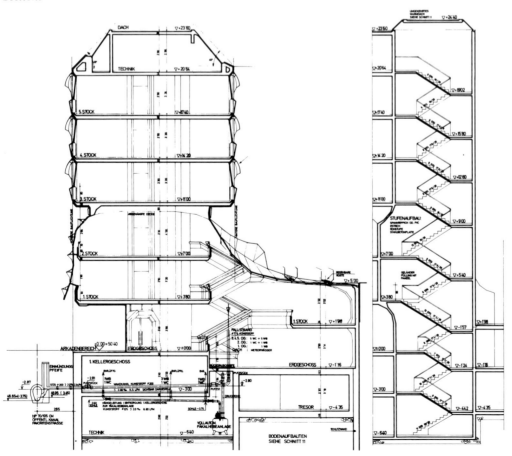

GÜNTHER DOMENIG

Stone House ▪ Steindorf, Carinthia ▪ 1986–present

Composite ground floor plan/axonometric

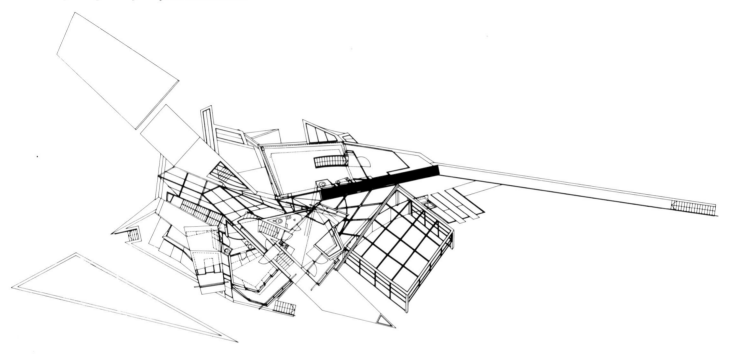

Domenig's design process is extremely personal; he believes that understanding originates in the projection of personal emotions onto the world of objects. His initial drawings are usually quite naive—essential forms unencumbered by technical considerations. Through a careful transition Domenig gives the forms a more concrete buildable shape. The forms eventually depart from their natural relationships, but Domenig continuously searches for a systematic order that retains the organic complexity of the sketches.

The Stone House offered Domenig his first opportunity to draw upon this personal design tradition, since he had lived in Steindorf with his family and brought to the project a deep understanding of the natural and cultural context of the site. The idea began with the surrounding hills, which cascade down with rocks and boulders breaking out of them. Domenig emphasized the transition between the two zones of vegetation and rock. This was not a conscious attempt literally to translate the landscape into architecture, but a desire, perhaps even an anxiety, to balance the natural environment with man-made form. Next followed a phase of practical experimentation that reveals Domenig's technical and engineering skills.

The project is complex and not confined to a singular entity; Domenig considers it a communal house, a collective atelier, a place that condenses and focuses his life's memories. This imploded expression is charged with personal meaning, yet open to be experienced by other personal histories that enhance the multiple identities of the place. An inspired source of life for this project is the well of light and water around which the plan spirals. Windows do not detract from the spaces; they are not holes in planes but voids resulting from partial volumes.

51

Composite elevation/section/perspective

West

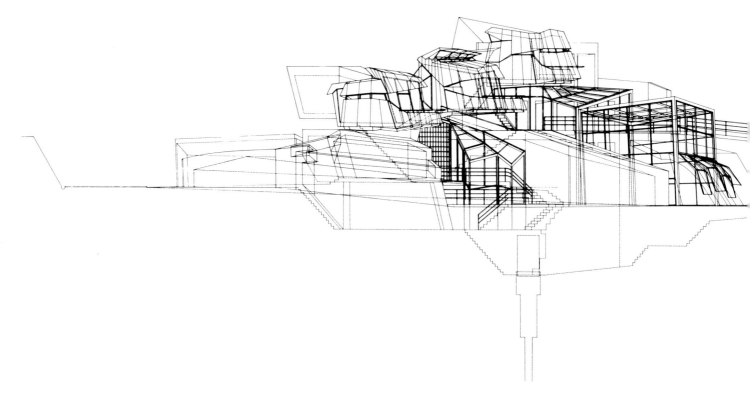

East

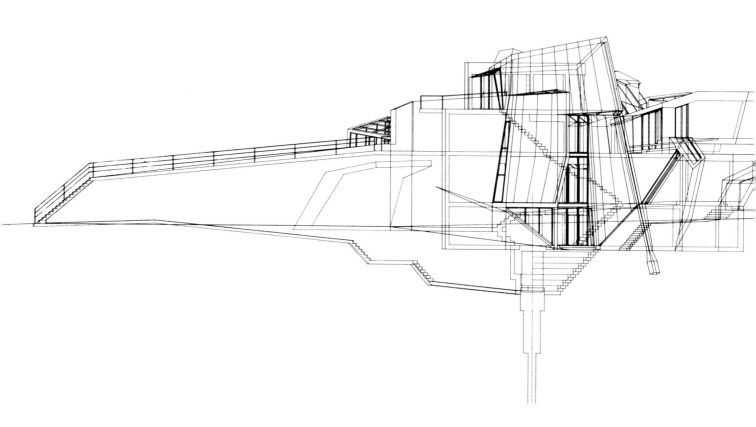

North

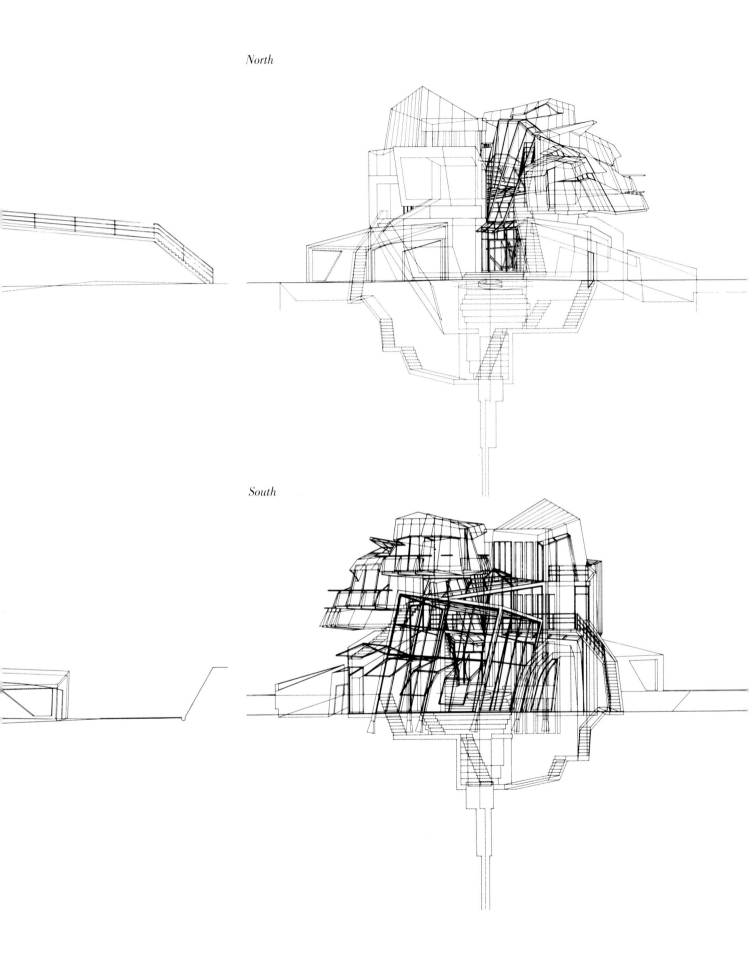

South

Architecture and landscape
Architecture and the site
Architecture and the idea
The one site
grass and stone
The other site
open and soft
The subjective dimensions of the site
The site as memory
The site as experience
The site as representation
The site as self-representation

Hills rise from the ground
rocks burst through
They are separated by an abyss
The rocks are metal
and the hills are walls
Spaces and paths
leading below the water table
cut through them
Deep down in the basement
the spiral staircase
the arrow
and the water emerging from the ground
in the stationary pond in the floating
rocks dreams also
come piggyback
The abyss is where one walks
the cube where one meets
the wedge where one eats
The low path under the water
to the water
the high path
to the water
and into the water
Breaking out
getting ready
to break through

Günther Domenig

DRIENDL*STEIXNER

Platform Office/Apartment ▪ Salzgries 15 ▪ Vienna ▪ 1988

Not all of Driendl*Steixner's endeavors are what would typically be considered architecture. For this team, video and film have served as alternate media for exploring current concerns.

This office/apartment in Vienna occupies an entire level, filled with novel design ideas that reflect Driendl*Steixner's broad interests. Restructuring the existing apartment enabled the client, an art historian, to embrace a totally new way of living while remaining in the same building he has occupied for fourteen years. The space was emptied of all that was unnecessary, then divided into three parts. One part is for living, marked by a stone floor; two parts are for working, marked by a wood floor. Such inventions as a prototypical door that closes in three directions emphasize this tripartite division. Each of the three adjoining rooms can assume three different configurations; in effect, one door creates nine different rooms.

On the facade, the signs of modern intervention are clear in the form of suspended projections and a swinging flower box.

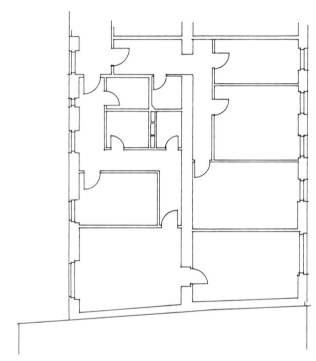

Original floor plan

Current floor plan

1 Entrance
2 Foyer
3 Open kitchen
4 Dining area
5 Living area I
6 Living area II
7 Sleeping area
8 Bathroom
9 Shower and toilet

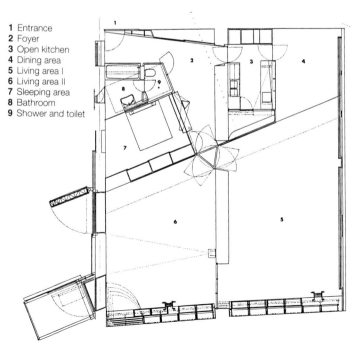

North elevation

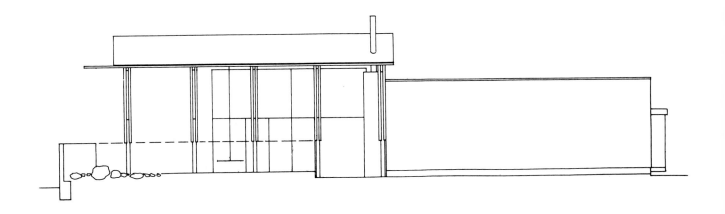

South elevation

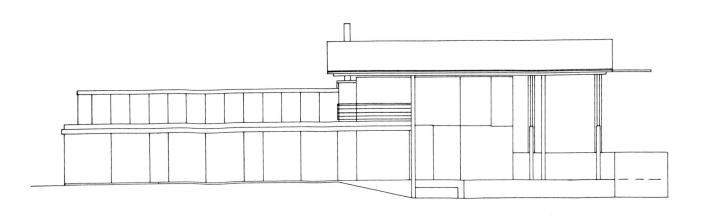

West elevation

East elevation

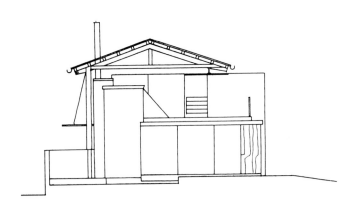
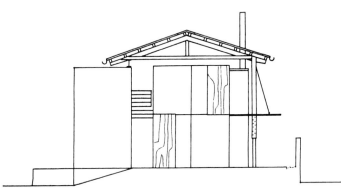

EICHINGER ODER KNECHTL

Truman's Shoe Shop ▪ Salzburg ▪ 1990
Wrenkh Vegetarian Restaurant and Bar ▪ Vienna ▪ 1989

Gregor Eichinger and Christian Knechtl have been working on urban issues since 1982, when they held the first organized meeting of the Rastlos ("restless") group of young architects and designers. The group reconvened in 1989 to work on urban studies centered in the Mariahilfer district of Vienna. One such project proposed a constructive use for a long-standing abandoned antiaircraft tower built during World War II.

The focus of Eichinger oder ("or") Knechtl's work has been the search for a productive form for the future. Their investigations into design encompass not only architecture and interiors but also graphics, exhibition spaces, furniture, and video. The team's deeply rooted cultural understanding of architecture prevents the work from becoming domineering in the sense of expressing only one point of view. Their designs emphasize the user, and their work seems slightly ahead of its time and addresses itself to a global audience.

Truman's Shoe Shop incorporates materials and objects that are appropriate to both new and old buildings: concrete, aluminum shelves, sliding panels, and back-lit glass. Floor materials—asphalt, carpeting, wood, concrete, and stone—simulate the city's varied walking surfaces.

The Wrenkh Bar displays considerable elegance and finesse behind a facade of steel and angled glass. Its broad-grained terrazzo floors attract the most attention, while the rest of the restaurant dons a quieter demeanor. The walls are covered with warm-colored wood panels that can be made to glow as they swing out and allow the recessed lighting to work its magical effects. A floor-to-ceiling sheet of glass mounted on tracks in front of the bar announces the daily menu.

Facing page and above:
Truman's Shoe Shop

Left: Wrenkh Vegetarian Restaurant and Bar

Right: Rastlos Music Cafe and Bar

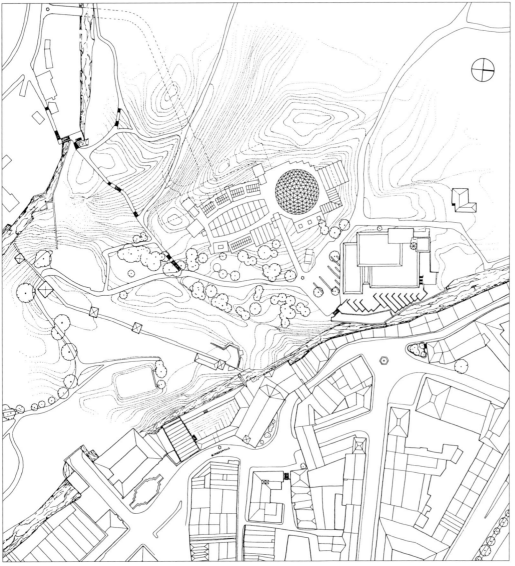

Upper level plan

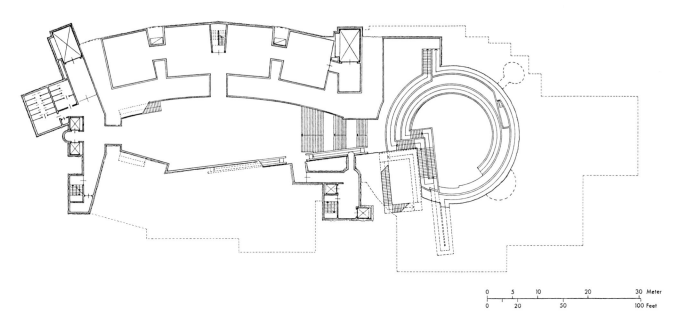

0 5 10   20   30 Meter
0   20   50   100 Feet

Sections

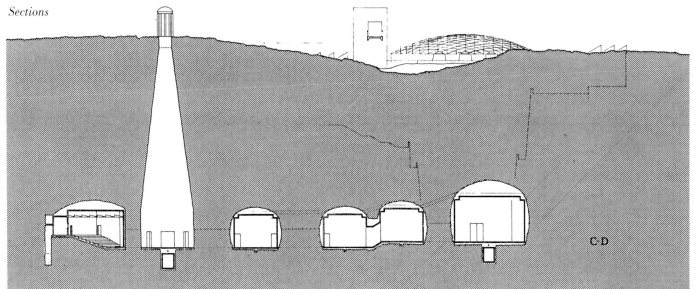

C-D

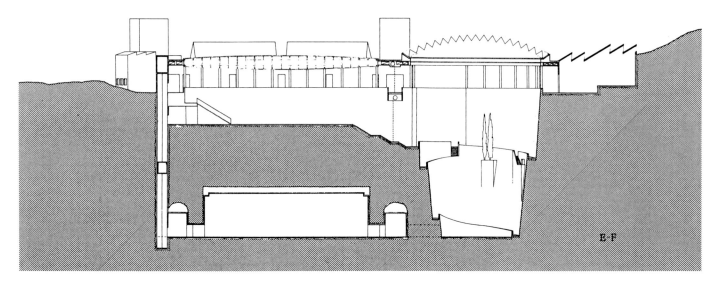

E-F

HANS HOLLEIN

Haas Haus ▪ Vienna ▪ 1990

The center of Vienna requires architectural solutions that are significantly contextual, placing great demands on new construction. Vienna's long evolution has produced no perfect urban solution, and designs that confront major issues still are not easily achieved in this historic city. Hans Hollein's Haas Haus addresses some of the long-standing deficiencies of the open spaces of Stephansplatz, Stock im Eisen-Platz, and links to the Graben (a pedestrian promenade).

Stock im Eisen-Platz provides a poorly defined connection between Stephansplatz and the Graben area. Because of the subway structures below, few design options were available. The Haas Haus's rounded facade originated from the curved form of Roman structures below. A setback in the building facade, together with a projecting element, create tension between Stock im Eisen-Platz and Stephansplatz. This projection establishes a definite corner for Stephansplatz, visually connecting it to the cathedral. The Haas Haus also serves as a termination point to the Kärntnerstrasse axis.

The building interior reveals a similar multiplicity and layering of functions. Fourteen shops and small eating areas are connected through an atrium extending more than five floors. This atrium is set back at ground level and is accessible through passages from both the Stock im Eisen-Platz/Stephansplatz and the Graben. Above the atrium are three levels of offices, crowned by a restaurant with an exquisite view of the city and cathedral. Although the cathedral remains the focus around which everything centers in this area, individual buildings appear as singular constructs, marked by their respective styles, epochs, and purposes. Haas Haus's highly differentiated silhouette takes into account the expressive roof shapes of the surrounding buildings.

The nontectonic, membranelike material used on the curved facade facing the Graben is reinforced by the diagonal pattern of the stone, offering yet another transition element from the Graben to Stephansplatz. The Graben's dominant fenestration patterns are reflective and smoothly terminated in a stepped composition on this facade. The facade on Goldschmiedgasse, an adjacent street, recalls elements of the cathedral in its structuring and massing.

Ground floor plan

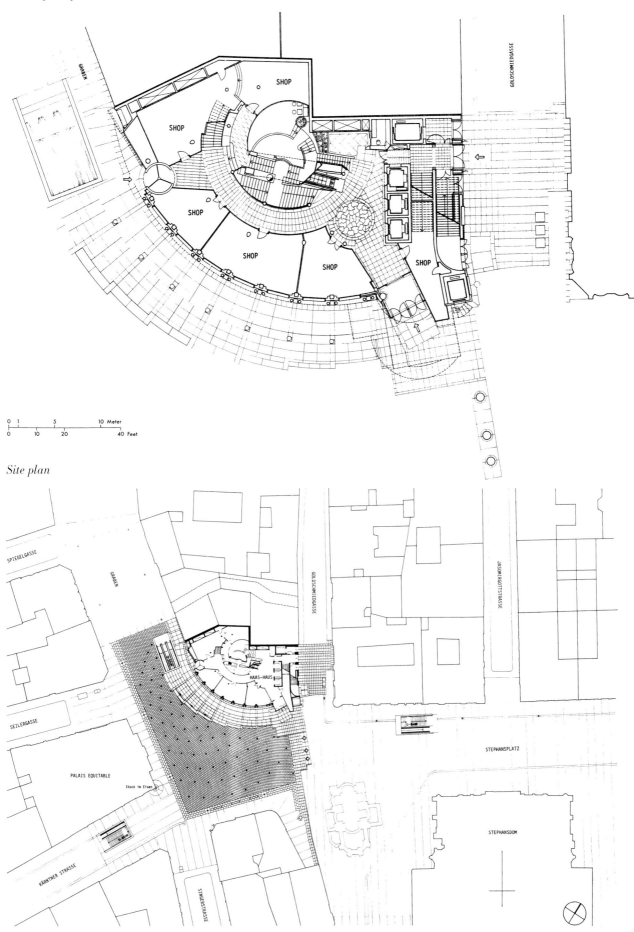

SHOP

SHOP

SHOP

SHOP

SHOP

SHOP

GRABEN

GOLDSCHMIEDGASSE

0 1   5   10 Meter
0   10   20   40 Feet

Site plan

SPIEGELGASSE

GRABEN

SEILERGASSE

PALAIS EQUITABLE

Stock im Eisen

KÄRNTNER STRASSE

SINGERSTRASSE

GOLDSCHMIEDGASSE

HAAS-HAUS

JASOMIRGOTTSTRASSE

STEPHANSPLATZ

STEPHANSDOM

Ground floor plan

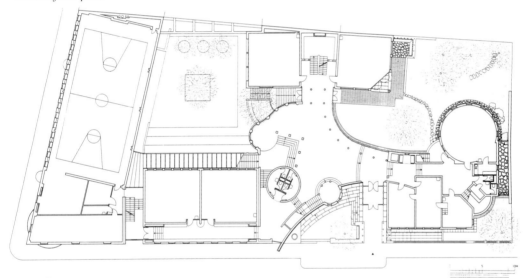

Site plan

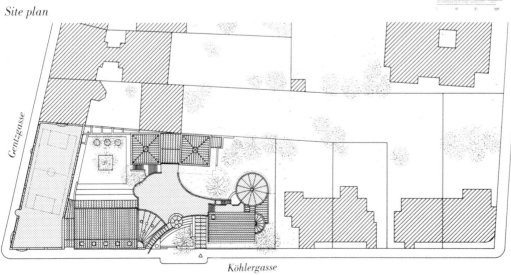

Gentzgasse

Köhlergasse

Longitudinal section

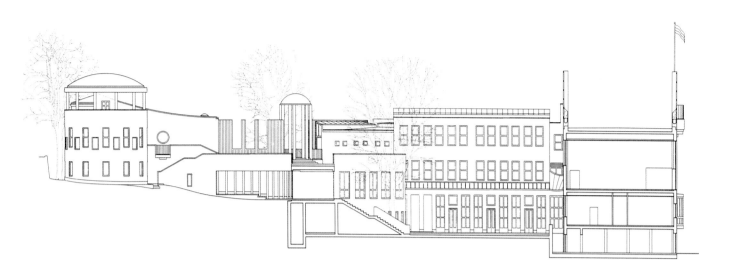

Gentzgasse elevation

Cross section through stairway

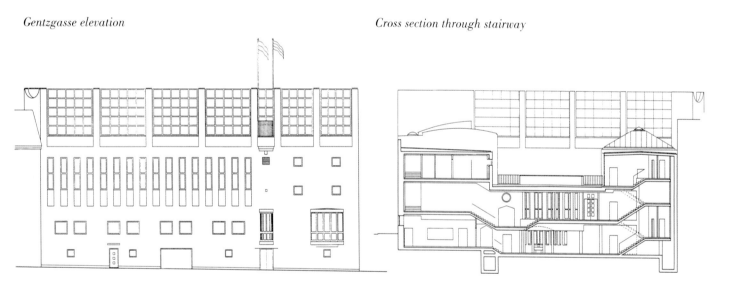

Köhlergasse elevation

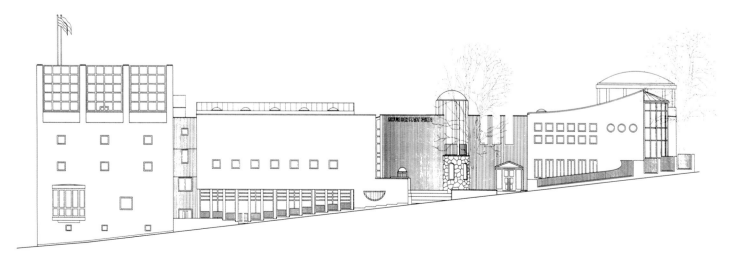

91

WILHELM HOLZBAUER

Faculty of Natural Sciences, University of Salzburg • Salzburg • 1986
(with H. Marschalek, H. Ekhart, G. Ladstätter, St. Hübner)

In designing the University's Faculty of Natural Sciences, Holzbauer sought an architectural expression congenial to Salzburg's rich historical tradition, yet unmistakably modern. The resulting architectural language is specific rather than universal: the plan relates to the surroundings of this particular site and is not interchangeable. The language is mannered and picturesque. Functions define the form, but the formal concept is interpreted pragmatically.

Certain elements of Salzburg's urban structure are quoted intentionally in a sort of *maniera salisburgensis*. Courtyards use measurements and proportions similar to those of the *Fürstenstadt*, the Salzburg of archbishops and dukes. Other architectural features, such as the circular entrance court with the sloping floor, have deliberately exaggerated formal aspects. Urban components also display intentional contrast: the facade is traditional, a plastered surface with windows set almost flush. A small interruption in the facade widens to a forecourt. Behind a second narrowing the wide, circular space of the entry court opens up, adding surprise and drama to this succession of spaces. A massive, freestanding gate in front of a glass wall at the center of the complex marks the main entrance.

Holzbauer's project reinterprets the tradition of small palaces and manor houses with formal and informal entrances that commonly employ walls, courtyards, and gates. The street facades of the Faculty building, interrupted only at the entry point, differ from the west elevation, which faces an open landscape accented by the water castle Freisaal in its center and the monumental fortress of Hohensalzburg in the distance.

The design also juxtaposes massive and transparent volumes, "traditional" and "modern." A glass-enclosed hall extending up through all floors provides the focus of the entire complex. Extensive glazed surfaces of the "palm houses," or conservatories, that extend over almost the entire length of the building are a backdrop for a composition of different forms and volumes. These include terraces, picturesque cubes, and the open-air theater. Together these elements make a gradual transition from architecture into landscape. Newly created ponds in the foreground and the existing clusters of trees and rows of poplars are integrated into the overall composition.

WILHELM HOLZBAUER

IBM Headquarters ▪ Vienna ▪ 1991

The IBM building is part of a complex of three office buildings whose varying shapes and heights were determined by an urban planning competition organized by the city in 1979. The complex was part of a plan to extend Vienna's urban boundaries closer to the Danube river by promoting construction in the less-developed Prater area. The United Nations Center and the recently completed Vienna Conference Center are part of this plan.

IBM wished to consolidate its operations in a single building that would incorporate functions previously scattered across seven buildings in the inner city. The new site at the Prater Stern, an entertainment district in Vienna, is well connected to public and private transportation systems and is minutes away from both the inner city and the airport.

The firm considered it necessary to include the most advanced technology in the project whenever possible. Because one third of an employee's life typically is spent in the working environment, IBM felt that design must direct and motivate the individual worker. Every effort was made to insure optimum working conditions for the employees while incorporating the program requirements into a specific form that would convey a positive corporate identity.

IBM required an unusually large number of small, single-person offices, each with a window. In response to this great demand for exterior wall space, large open courtyards were cut into the building mass, allowing views toward the parklike landscape of the Prater. In anticipation of future construction on adjacent sites, the building's facades align with the street, generating boulevards for the twenty-first century.

The approach to the entrance hall is under a delicate roof structure extending toward Lassallestrasse and the subway entrance. The entrance hall provides access to the training area, which contains classrooms and group meeting rooms. The first level above the ground floor opens to the training area below. Located on this level is the cafeteria and kitchen, dining room, coffee shop, bank, and travel office. The upper floors connect through stairs in a glass-enclosed atrium, encouraging nonmechanical travel from floor to floor.

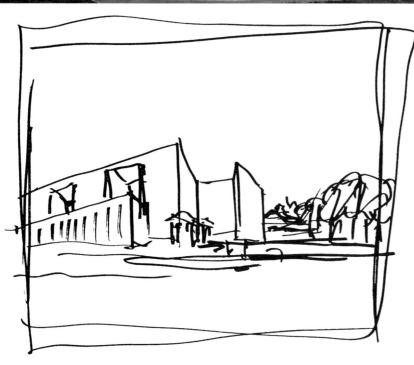

WILHELM HOLZBAUER

Schmid House, Im Gereute 1a ▪ Vienna ▪ 1992

This characteristic Holzbauer project reveals his skillful pragmatism on a small scale. The Schmid House is based on a square in which an L-shaped form containing the interior spaces wraps around a square courtyard. The court is bordered on the west side by an arcade, with the dominant view to the south framed by the large portal. Within the court, the kitchen and dining room terrace is partly covered by a second-level balcony. The remaining courtyard area contains vegetation, integrating the garden and the house.

There are two levels above ground and one below, providing this house with an open, free-flowing quality. The ground floor contains common spaces such as the entrance foyer, kitchen, and dining and living areas. A gallery spanning the two-story living room connects the ground floor with the upstairs bedrooms by a staircase. The garage is incorporated within the house, eliminating awkward structural appendages.

Mezzanine level plan

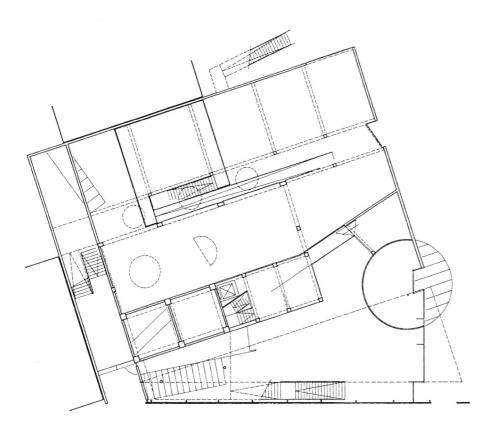

Site plan

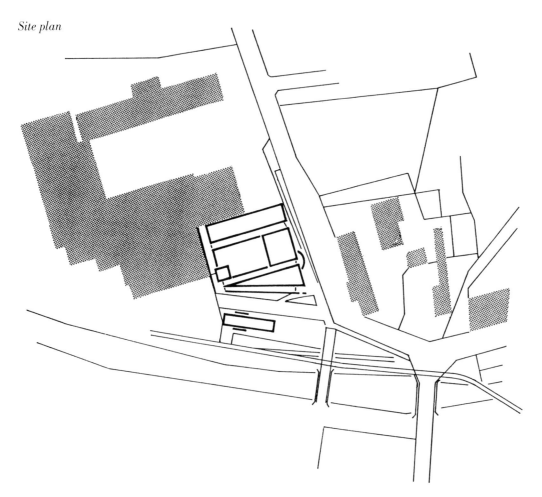

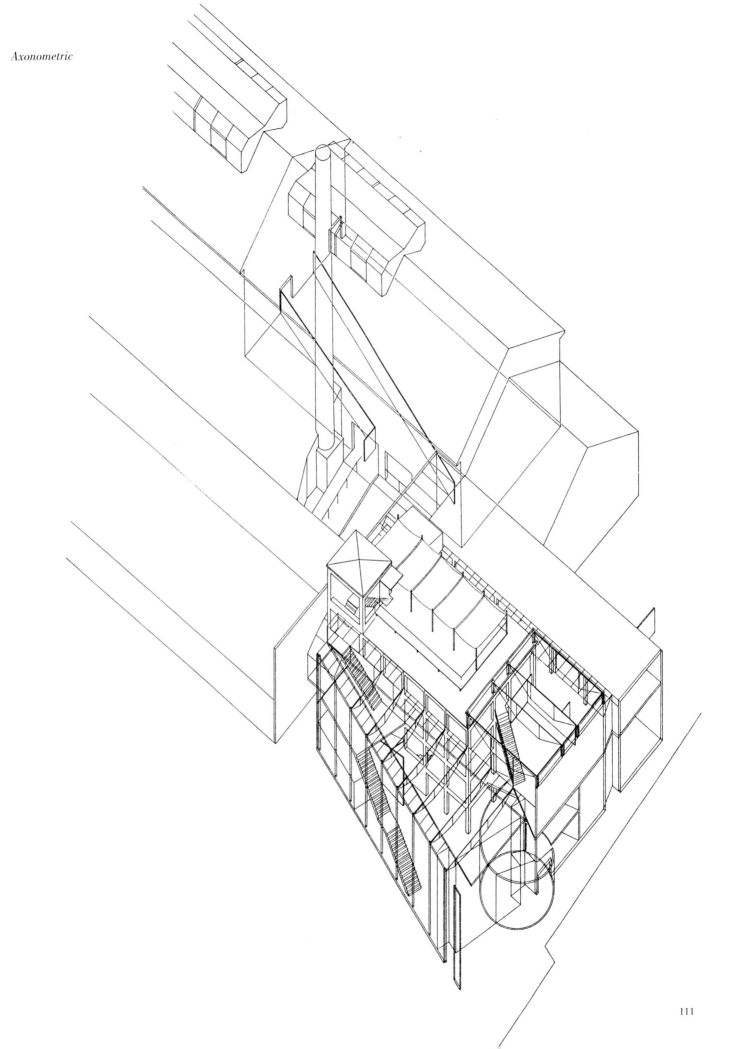

Exhibition area plan

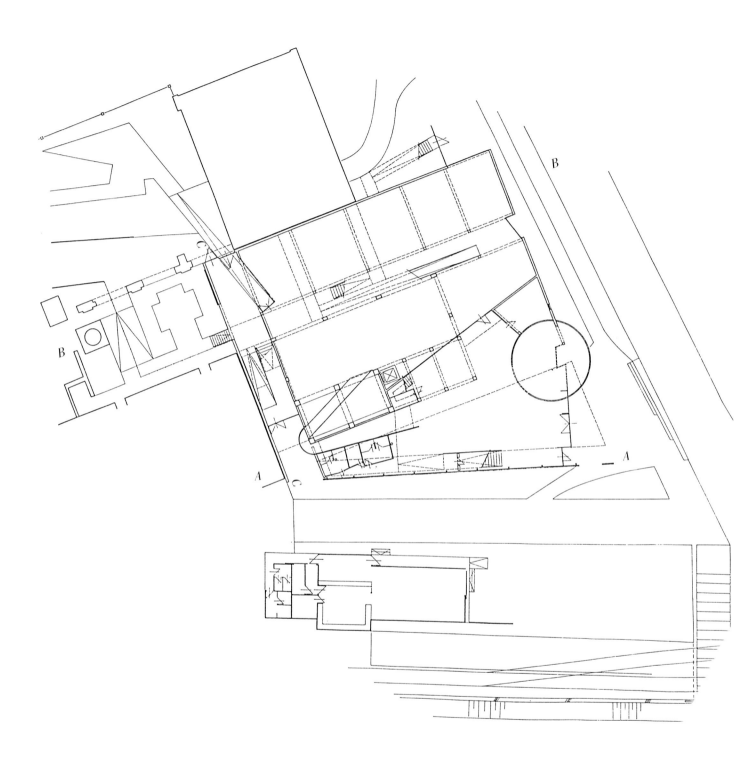

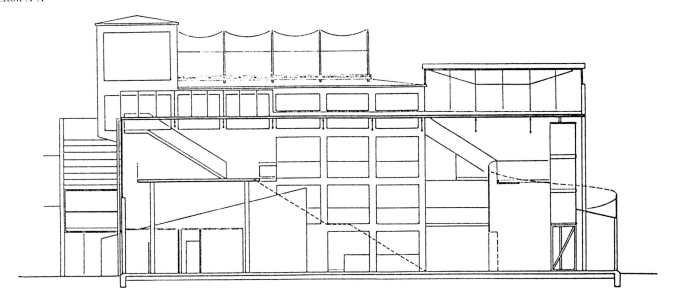

Section A-A

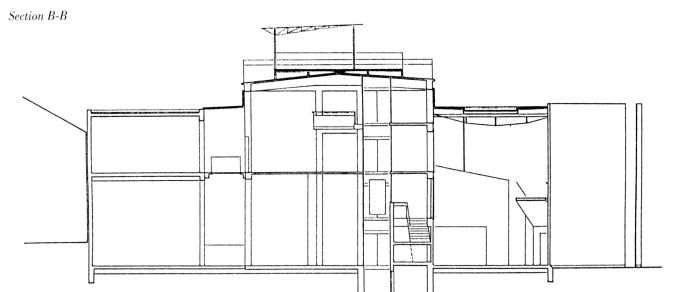

Section B-B

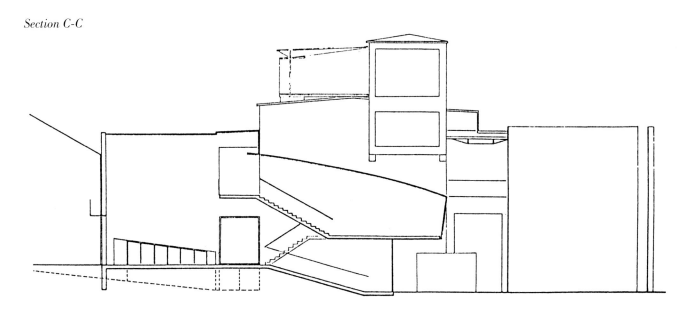

Section C-C

115

KLAUS KADA

WIST Student Housing ▪ Graz ▪ 1991

At the periphery of the city, and therefore somewhat removed from traffic noise, Klaus Kada proposed a courtyard building scheme that provides variable access while ensuring uniform lighting and exposure to daylight. This project is based on a traditional building typology quite prevalent in Graz.

Two parallel building volumes enclose a courtyard in the northeast corner of the site. An existing seven-story building was extended with a terraced addition that divides the site into public and semipublic spaces. Along this axis is the access to all buildings.

Access from the Wienerstrasse (southwest) to the court follows both property lines to join the interior, perpendicular axis. This intersection contains the vertical circulation elements. Horizontal circulation at the upper levels is through galleries (open, single-loaded corridors) that provide a transition from public to private areas and allow for the extension of individual living units.

Most of the living units are two stories high. Single-occupancy rooms face the quiet side, away from the access galleries. Each unit has at least one open area or terrace.

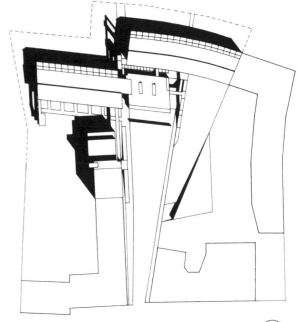

Ground floor plan

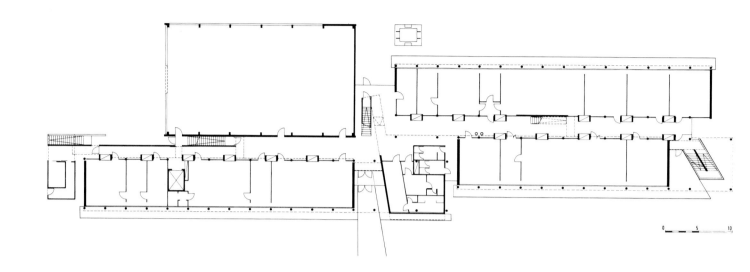

North elevation

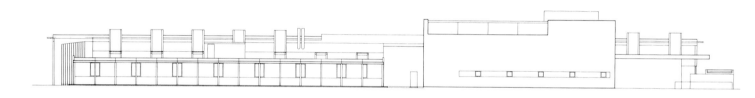

South elevation

East elevation

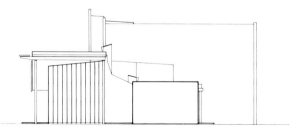

West elevation

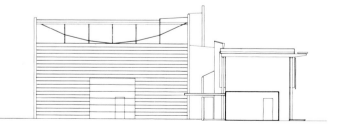

ROB KRIER

Housing Complex, Schrankenberggasse 18–20 ▪ Vienna ▪ 1987

This asymmetrical site suggested division into two separate sites, each symmetrical onto itself. Two buildings were designed as unconnected structures, allowing each to act independently of the other. The more prominent corner building furthers this intent with symmetrical facades and floor plans. The largest units are logically located in this building. Both solar-sensitive buildings face a green courtyard that receives southern sunlight.

In public housing projects, budgetary restraints and other priorities often override many of the architect's more enriching design elements. Many of Krier's ideas were ultimately excluded in this project's execution. These include special entrances, more elaborate stair towers, special cladding details, and intricate decoration on the main entrance.

Below: Living room perspective

Right: Elevations and plans

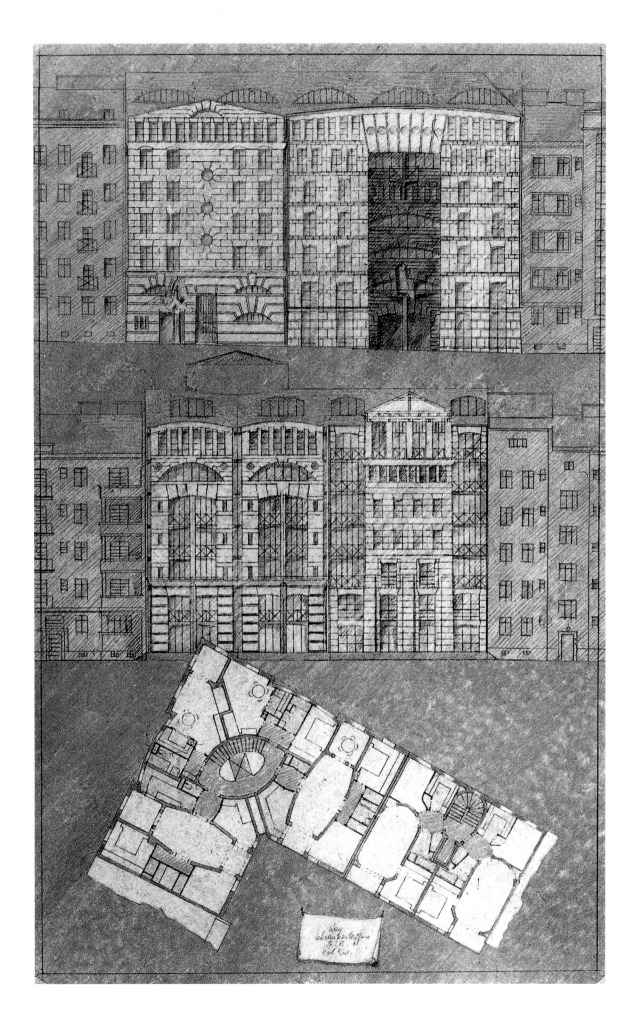

ROB KRIER

Housing Complex, Breitenfurterstrasse 401–413 ▪ Vienna ▪ 1988

Contemporary architecture in Vienna does not always express itself as one might expect. The city's architectural legacy encourages the opinion that buildings must be responsible to their contexts, making it very difficult to abandon all historical references in Vienna.

When a contextual project does not directly contribute to the advancement of "modern" architecture, it is often quickly dismissed as simply good planning shaped by old perceptions of what architecture should look like. This is not to say, however, that such work does not have a place in the new Austrian architecture.

In the Breitenfurterstrasse housing complex, for example, an architectural language specific to Vienna meets the functional requirements of modern residential housing. The structure was defined by the terrain and the desire to create physical and aesthetic relationships to the surrounding context. While this project is part of a citywide renewal program initiated in the 1980s, it also represents Vienna's creative spirit and commitment to its social environment.

The site lies in the southern section of the city, in a valley between the slopes of the Maurer mountains. On the east is the River Liesing; the west is bordered by access

roads. An aqueduct providing drinking water to the city divides the site. A public competition determined the segmentation of the project into three distinct parts. Robert Krier was responsible for planning the two ends of the site and laying out the central courtyard. Hedwig Wachberger and Peter Gebhart were responsible for most of the three hundred housing units.

This project revives the successful tradition of Viennese housing, with emphasis on the large inner courtyards typical of such buildings. To make this distinctive three-part project cohere, Krier used a circular courtyard to connect buildings grouped around triangular and rectangular courts. The housing building on the north, at the top of the sloping site, became the project's representative building, separated from the others by the aqueduct. This building has two wings branching out from a cylindrical module. Inside are a kindergarten and facilities for servicing the neighborhood roads. The inner triangular space between the two wings features a smaller oval building, which is primarily used for classrooms.

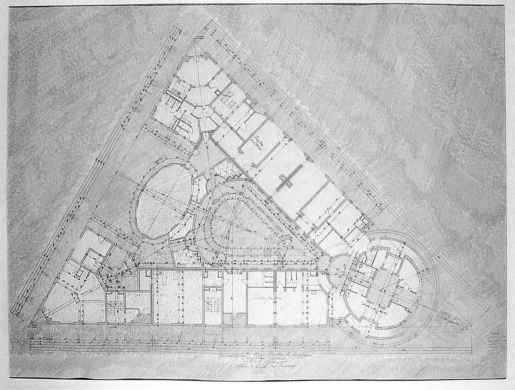

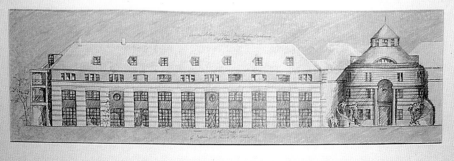

131

At the center of the complex is the circular courtyard,
thirty-two meters in diameter, which acts as the hub of the
overall plan and catalyzes social relationships in the
surrounding neighborhood. Several gateways lead into this
courtyard, named Camillo Sitte; shops and public areas
occupy a ground floor arcade. A raised platform
accommodates public performances such as short plays and
concerts. All of these activities occur around a central
fountain surrounded by monumental sculptures.

This project seeks to cultivate a formally and socially
self-sufficient neighborhood that still plays a vital role in
the city as it invites participation from the surrounding area.

ADOLF KRISCHANITZ

Traisen Pavilion ▪ St. Pölten, Lower Austria ▪ 1988

This exhibition pavilion, constructed in only two months, was to mark the birth of a new regional capital, St. Pölten. Two adjacent primary forms, a cylinder and a rectilinear slab, express a dual purpose of display and the display of architecture itself. The cylinder consists of twenty-four triple-height columns with galleries on three different levels inside. A suspended skylight diffuses daylight into the interior.

The adjoining slab is a vertical framework accessible by stairs and two levels of galleries. The south elevation is almost completely solid, while the north elevation, equipped with translucent panels, allows the necessary daylight for the exhibits.

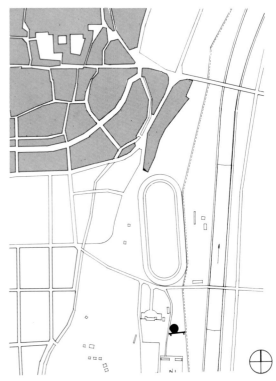

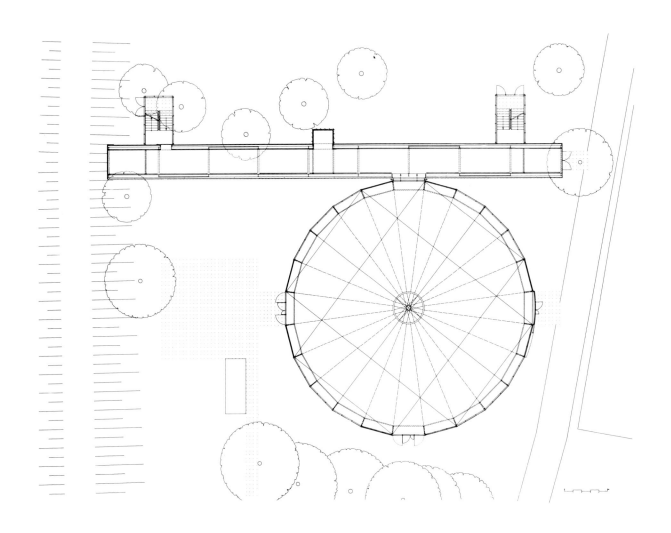

Perspective

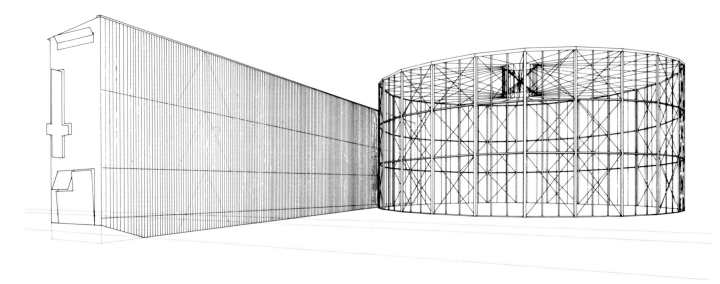

Section through rectilinear slab

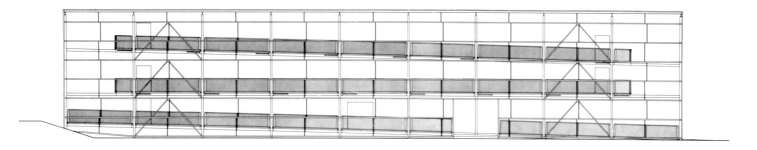

Elevation

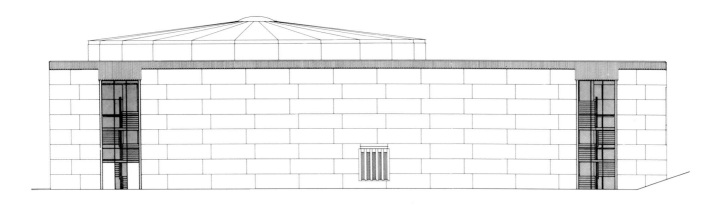

Section through cylinder

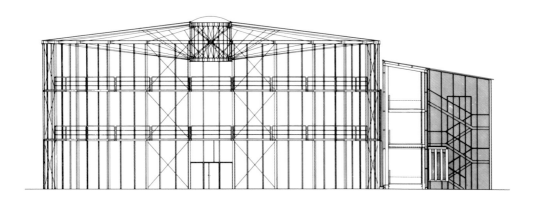

ADOLF KRISCHANITZ

Housing Complex, Pilotengasse / Hausefeldstrasse ▪ Vienna ▪ 1992
(with Herzog & de Meuron and Otto Steidle)

Adolf Krischanitz developed this project in association with Jacques Herzog and Pierre de Meuron (both from Basel), and Otto Steidle, from Munich. The development includes two hundred residential units. Krischanitz's section encompasses seventy-six units: thirteen detached single houses, five semidetached houses, two apartments, forty-two terraced houses, thirteen single garages and one underground parking garage.

His slightly curved rows of houses are located in the middle of the development. Pedestrian access paths fall in straight lines perpendicular to the housing, thus creating different spaces on each side of the building. These oscillating rows are also staggered along the longitudinal axis to form spatial sequences that open and close.

The building masses and exterior spaces are of equal importance, as together they create this changing spatial network. This interdependence of structures and open space is accentuated by graduated and contrasting color sequences.

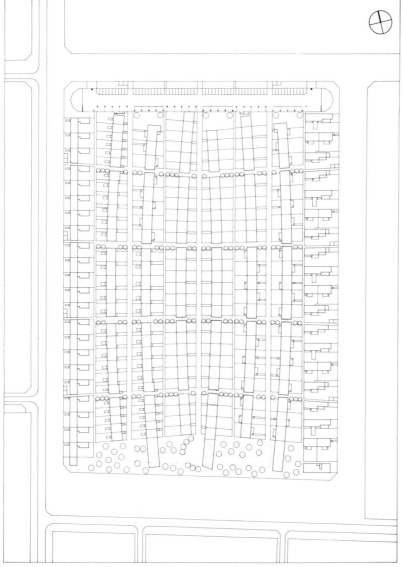

Ground floor plans, terraced houses

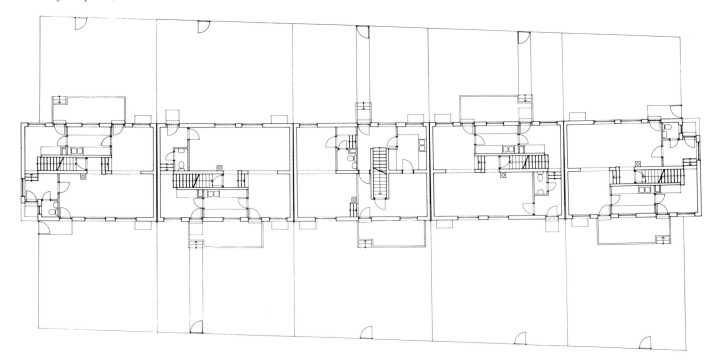

Typical elevation, terraced houses

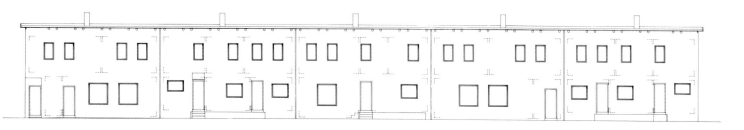

Typical section, terraced houses

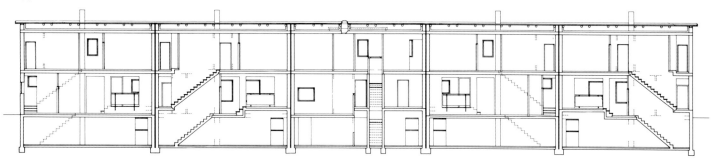

Elevations, detached house

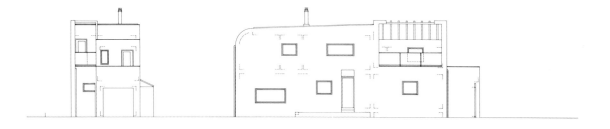

JOSEF LACKNER

Wüstenrot Insurance Headquarters ▪ Salzburg ▪ 1992

This innovative building represents a new generation of office buildings in which information is disseminated electronically and workstations meet computer users' ergonomic and light requirements. Although the building responds to the rational demands of an office building, the environmental and human dimensions are given exceptional attention.

Spatial transparency throughout the interior along with glazed exterior surfaces open up this corridorless building. The structural frame allows maximum flexibility and offers each office optimum lighting conditions.

The location adjacent to a main traffic artery complicated the design. A glass sound wall twelve meters high and eighty meters long shields the building from noise and pollution while retaining the view to the west. A formal tension between the curved mass of the office building and the sound wall results. The staggered concrete pylons of the sound wall will eventually be covered with planting to contrast with the glass reflections.

The site plan responds both to the scale of the automobile (on the street side) and the pedestrian (toward the sound wall). A tunnel below grade connects the main building to a garage and the street. Daylight is consistent throughout the building, including the first garage level below grade.

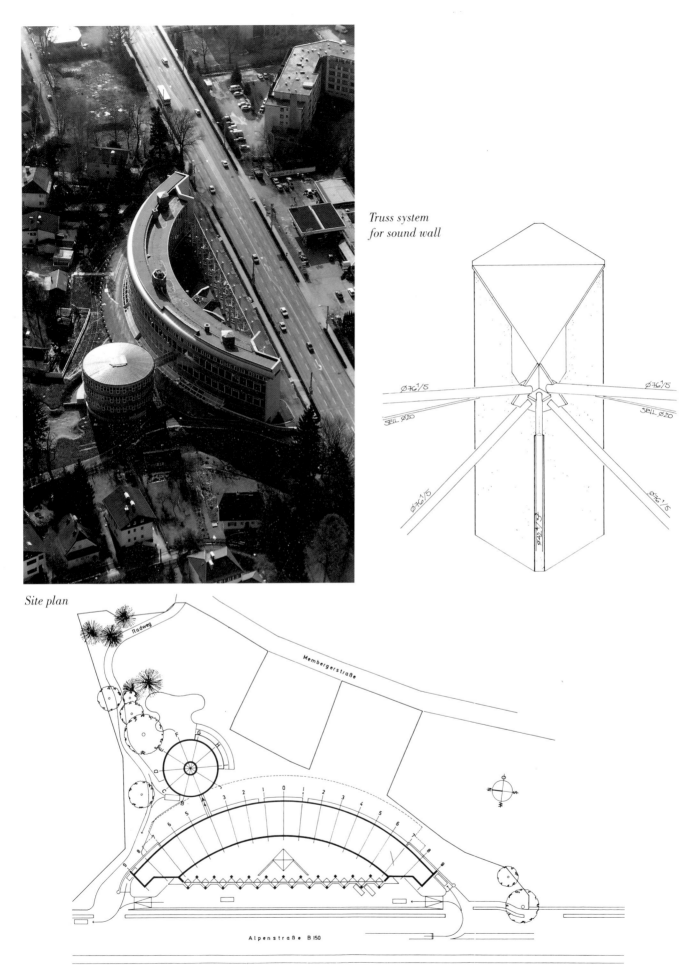

*Truss system
for sound wall*

Ø76¹/5
Ø76¹/5
SEIL Ø20
SEIL Ø20
Ø76¹/5
Ø76¹/5
Ø42¹/3

Site plan

Radweg

Membergerstraße

Alpenstraße B 150

Ground floor plan

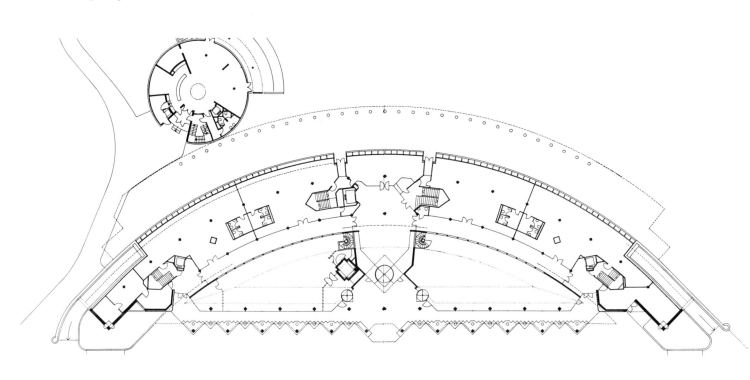

Section

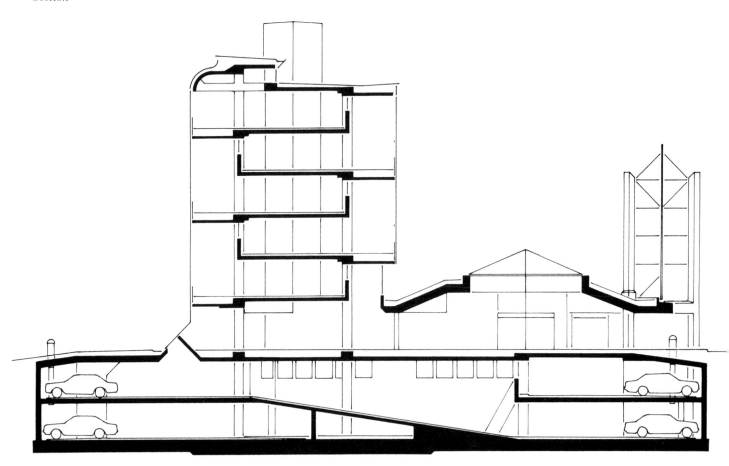

Ground floor plan

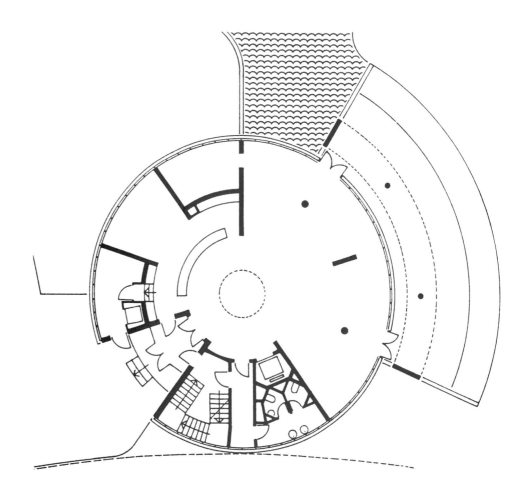

Section

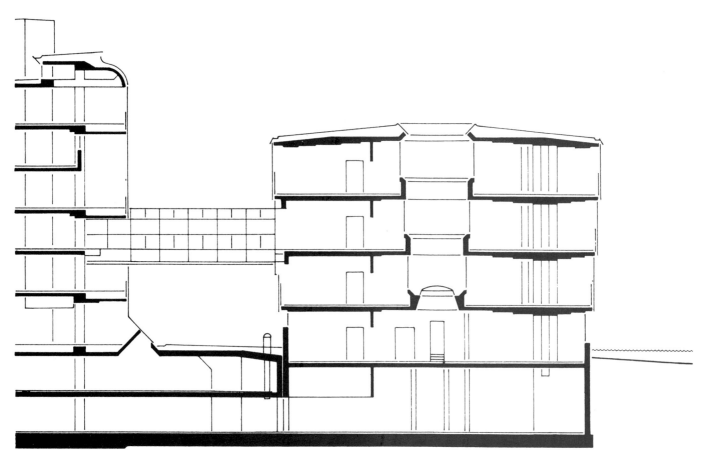

LAINER/AUER

Housing Complex, Hermanngasse 29 ▪ Vienna ▪ 1990

Ground floor plans, apartments

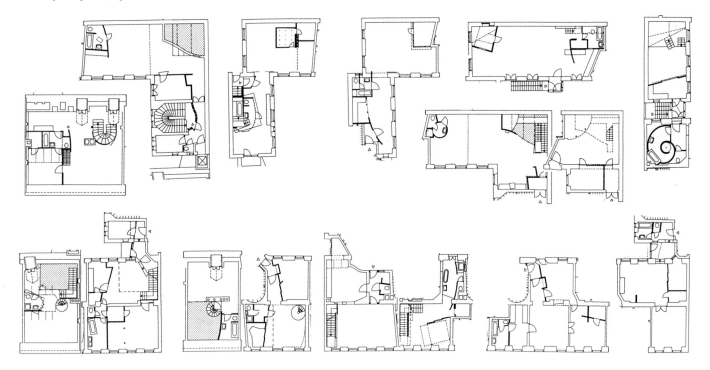

The architectural team of Rüdiger Lainer and Gertraud Auer made its initial impact on the Austrian architectural scene with this interior renovation of a landmark historic building (1825) and a four-story factory block behind it to the east. The interactive, participatory planning process was key in achieving diverse solutions instead of predictable variations in plan. The complex includes thirteen apartments, one commercial unit, and one professional practice.

The individual units are conceived as "landed elements," each deriving from its unique situation, shape, and chosen materials. Geometrically designed fields follow lines that act as "landing strips" to guide the placement of the different elements.

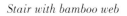

Stair with bamboo web

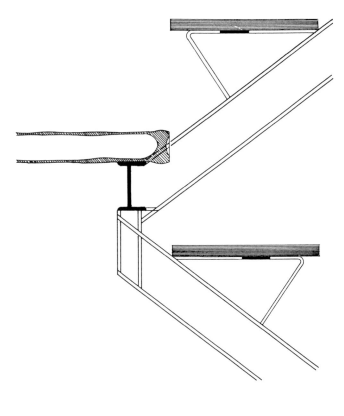

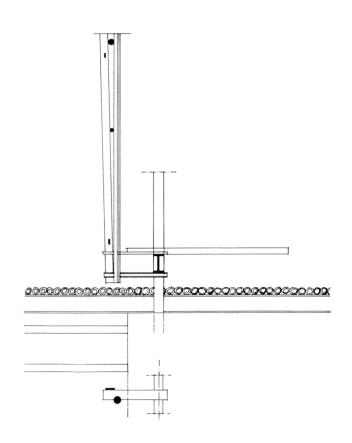

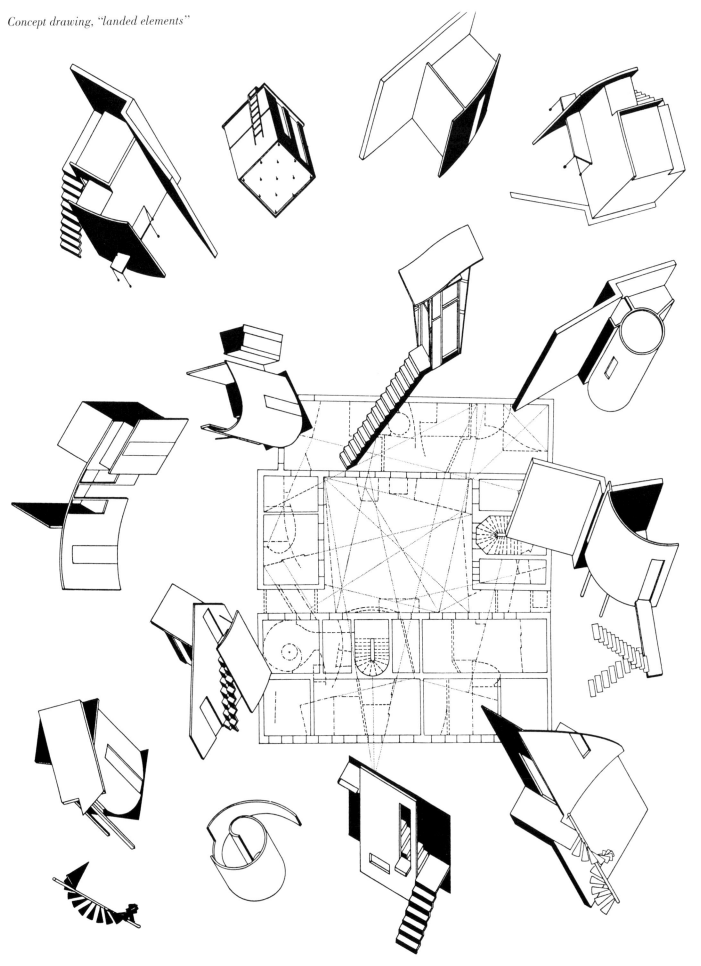

LAINER/AUER

Housing Complex, Waidhausenstrasse 24 ▪ Vienna ▪ 1991

This subsidized housing project is rich in contextual inspiration, reflecting the rhythm and tone of the neighboring buildings as well as the bend in the street. The architecture is dedicated to the occupants, creating an openness in keeping with the suburban ideal through two parallel wings and a children's playhouse in the courtyard between them.

The street line repeats in the building's subtly modulated shape. The wings, located along the edges of the site, create a quiet courtyard enlivened by articulated facades that echo the street. These courtyard facades dynamically interact with the open space they frame.

Room sizes and quality of interior spaces are consistent throughout the complex. The designers sought maximum flexibility by allowing a variety of combinations of units. Even the allocation of spaces for specific functions has been left open, so that the occupants may define their own living situations.

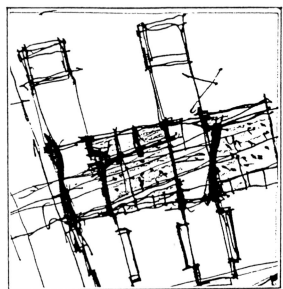

Street elevation

Courtyard elevation

ORTNER & ORTNER

Museum Quarter ▪ Vienna ▪ 1990–present

The Museum Quarter occupies the former Imperial Stables, converting this historic landmark into a compact city within a city. The project provides spaces for the Museum of Modern Art, an art gallery, library tower, and multipurpose hall. A museum of modern Austrian art and a media forum consisting of museums of film and photography are also planned.

Gottfried Semper's stately plan for a Viennese Imperial Forum, conceived in the late nineteenth century, placed the Imperial Stables (Fischer von Erlach, 1720) and the Neue Hofburg at either end of the main axis. Between these lay the two imperial museums (Natural History Museum and Museum of Fine Arts); the Maria Theresienplatz and the Burgtor, the former entrance to the castle, defined the transverse axis. The major axis extended all the way to the heart of the city, formally linking Vienna's high-density seventh district with the city center. In this new project the long facade of von Erlach's building separates the Imperial Forum from the city and cultural facilities behind.

The two significant contextual influences are the attention focused on the main entrance of von Erlach's building by the transverse axis of Semper's two museums, and the tenement quarters of the seventh district, which jut in at an angle from behind. These two directions serve as guidelines for the arrangement of buildings within the museum quarter. The projected intersection of the two axes creates an abundance of free spaces, each with a unique character. The largest single complex will be the Museum of Modern Art, a cube whose double shell of steel frame and glass will appear dark and solid in daylight, clear and transparent at night. Visible behind the long baroque facade of von Erlach's building, this structure will become a striking element of the skyline.

Ground floor plan

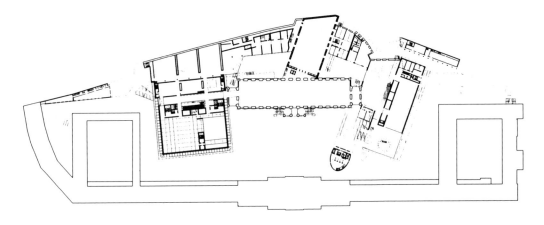

Section through Museum of Modern Art

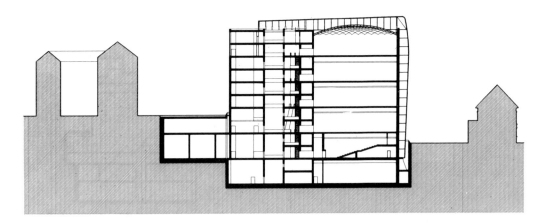

Section through multipurpose hall

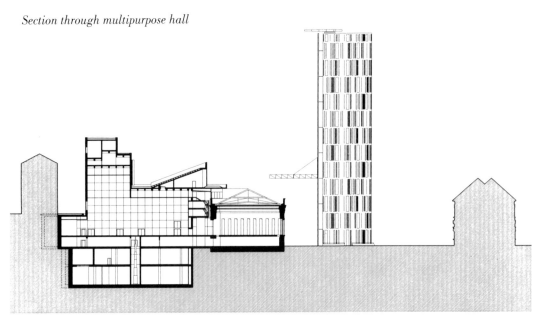

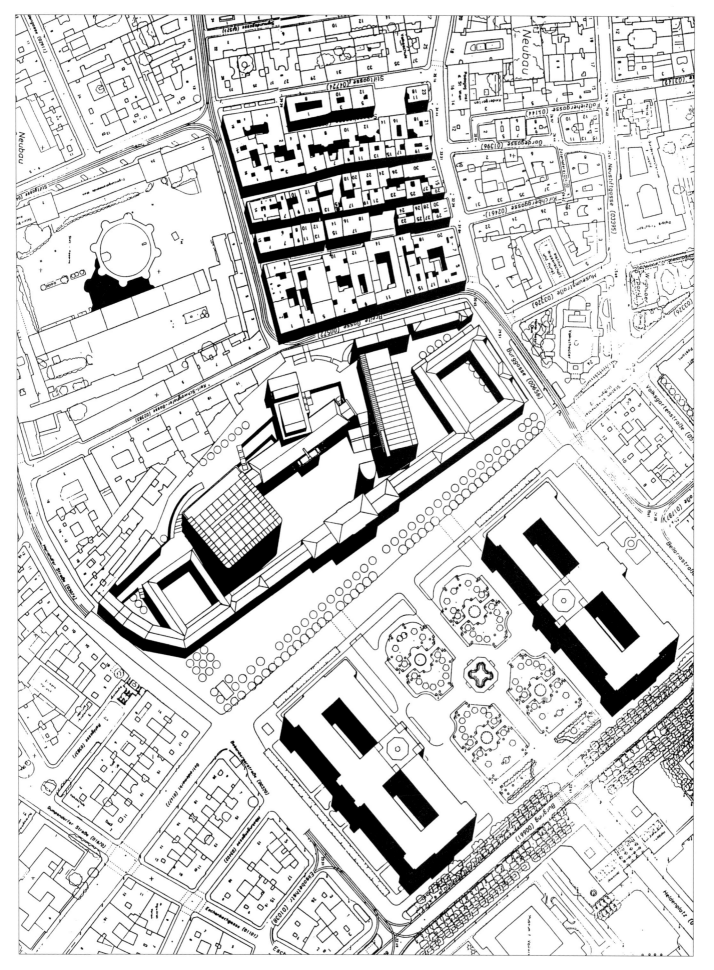

159

Elevation

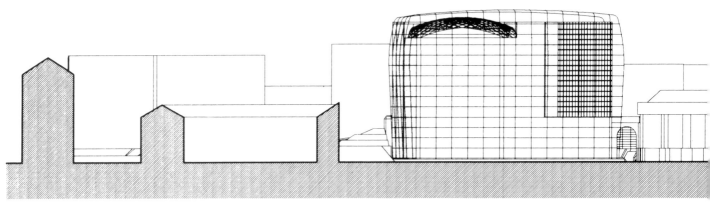

MUSEUM OF MODERN ART

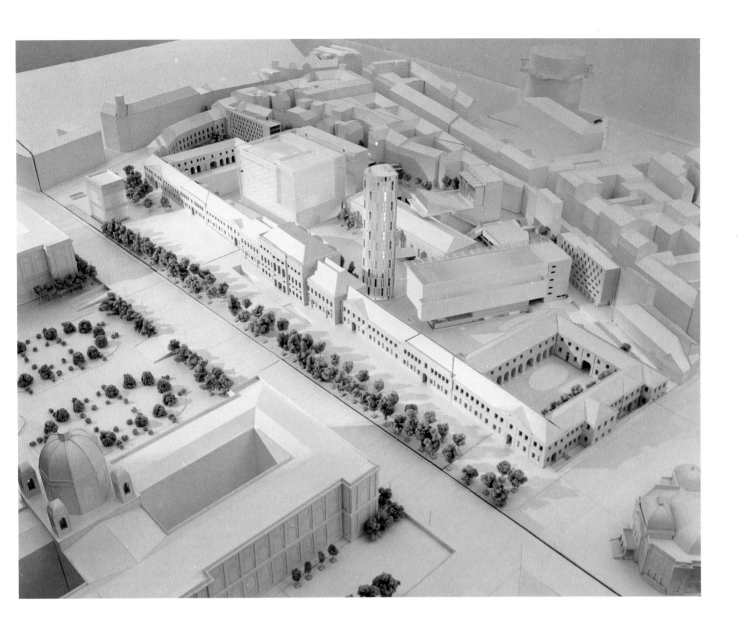

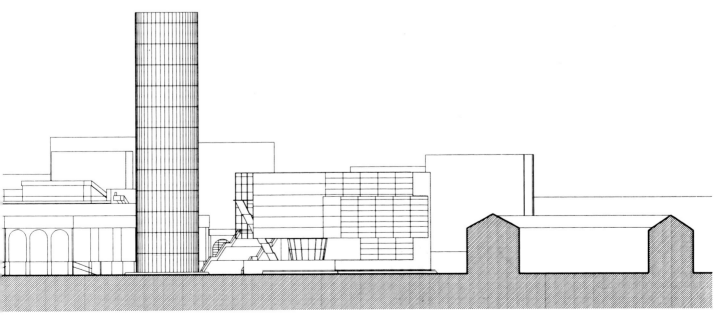

MULTIPURPOSE HALL   LIBRARY TOWER   ART GALLERY

GUSTAV PEICHL

ORF Broadcasting Studios ▪ Vienna ▪ 1983

The original complex of studios in Vienna for the Austrian Broadcasting Company was designed by Clemens Holzmeister in 1937. Peichl, along with Hans Hollein and Wilhelm Holzbauer, was a student of Holzmeister. These facilities, located in a typical urban area, currently house all of the television studios for Vienna and Lower Austria. In addition to the studios, there are rehearsal rooms, administrative offices, circulation, and storage areas. The site was completely occupied except for one sizable courtyard, which was to hold Peichl's 300,000-cubic-foot addition.

The new four-story complex connects at each level with the original building. The addition differentiates itself from the original through fenestration and color, without competing with Holzmeister's work. The meticulously detailed interior reveals a strong predilection for nautical motifs: railings, portals, and connecting bridges. Mechanical services have been integrated fluidly and effortlessly. During the two-year construction period, which included modernizing the existing facilities, broadcasting services functioned continuously.

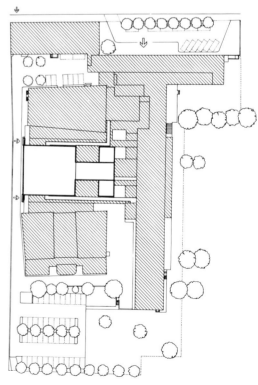

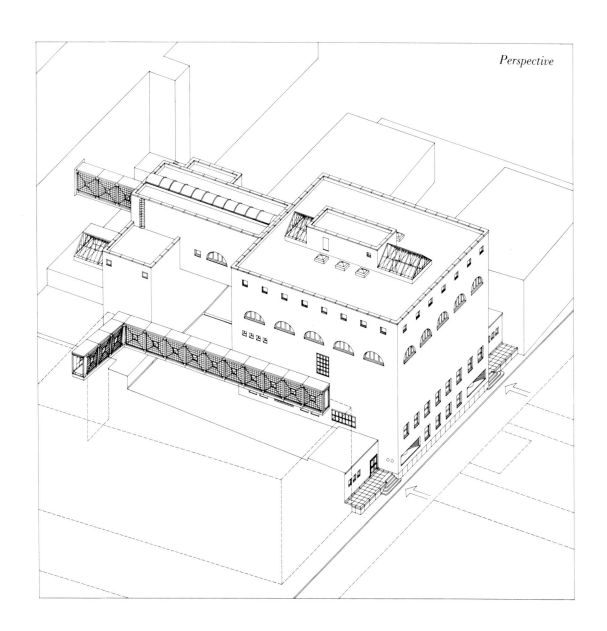

Perspective

Elevation

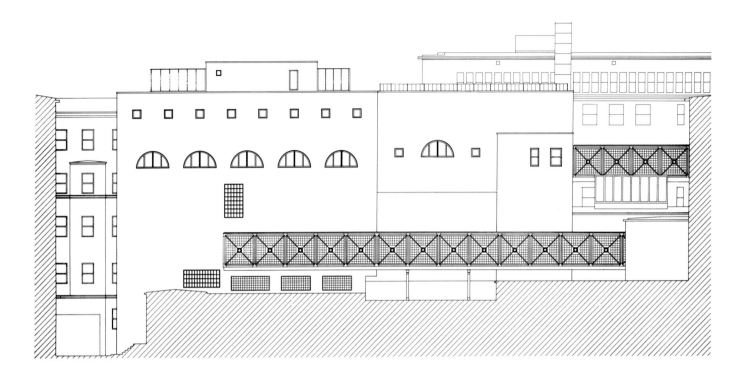

Front elevation

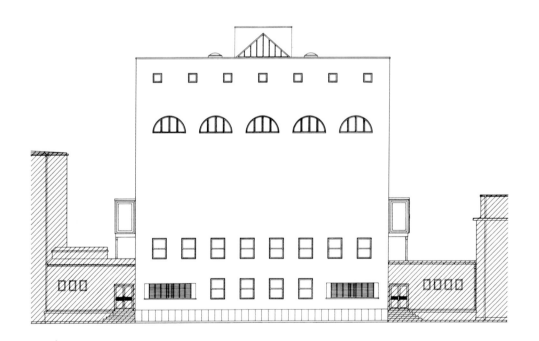

Perspective, central hall

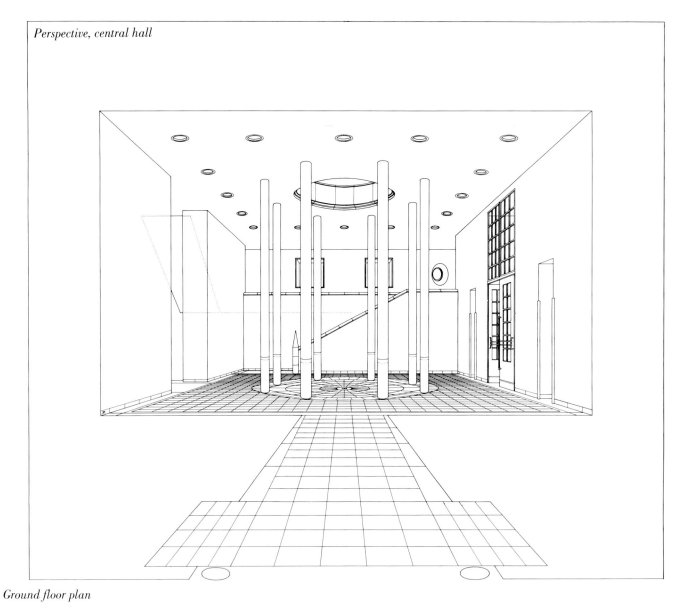

Ground floor plan

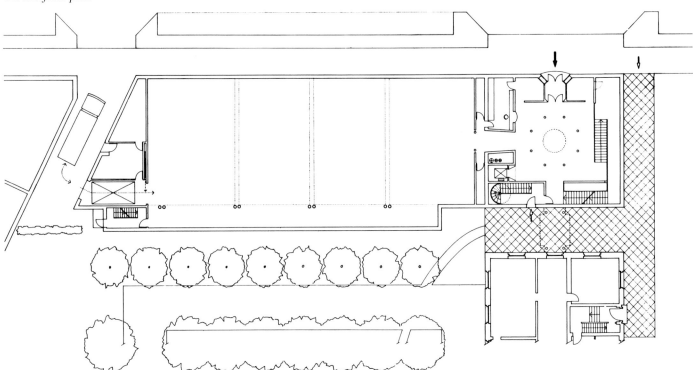

BORIS PODRECCA

KIKA Department Store ▪ Klagenfurt, Carinthia ▪ 1989

While inner-city buildings must be socially responsive, the outer areas of cities have long been regarded as wastelands, allowing and even perhaps encouraging less attractive, often monstrous structures to dominate. Little attention is given to good design and other enriching aspects that such structures might possess. Instead, synthetic and artificial devices such as advertisements, banners, and colors are employed to call attention to these buildings. The resulting structures are ugly, unsightly, and consequently reinforce their marginal status.

Boris Podrecca believes that these buildings must exploit a more sensitive vocabulary while retaining their large scale for economic reasons. When their monolithic size interferes with the city, urban form should prevail, and streets, passages, and galleries must be integrated. Such buildings would then fit into the city while better fulfilling their primary purpose. Podrecca searches for the urban context and poetic nature for the periphery that together would release these structures from blandness.

The KIKA department store reflects Podrecca's position. The building's structural integrity was of primary concern,

demanding a form representative of its construction method. The new construction, an expansion of the existing store, begins on the northeast end of the site with a continuous facade facing the Völkermarkterstrasse. The north facade is distinguished by three emergency stair towers built of steel and expanded metal, which mark the building's segmentation as it narrows toward a semicircular termination. The structure, with its prefabricated concrete elements, is crowned by a glazed lantern.

A glass tower, occupied by the main staircase, connects the new and old sections of this project. The upward spiral of these stairs concludes at a small café-pavilion crowning the tower and providing views of the surrounding area. At night the tower serves as a lighted beacon marking the entrance to the city. A diagonal axis from the stair tower across a small stone piazza terminates with a fountain immediately adjacent to the parking area. A new facade was laid over the existing structure to better articulate the urban context. In the gap between the two structures a metal net suspended from reinforced concrete columns allows views of the original facade.

Perspective from southeast

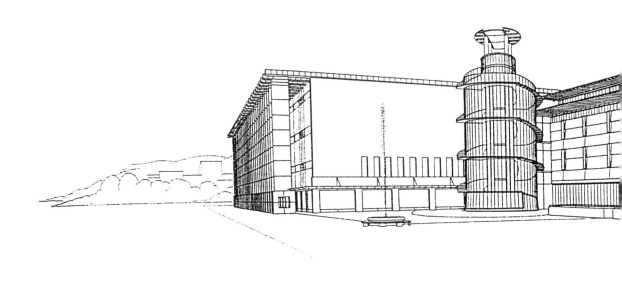

Perspective from northeast

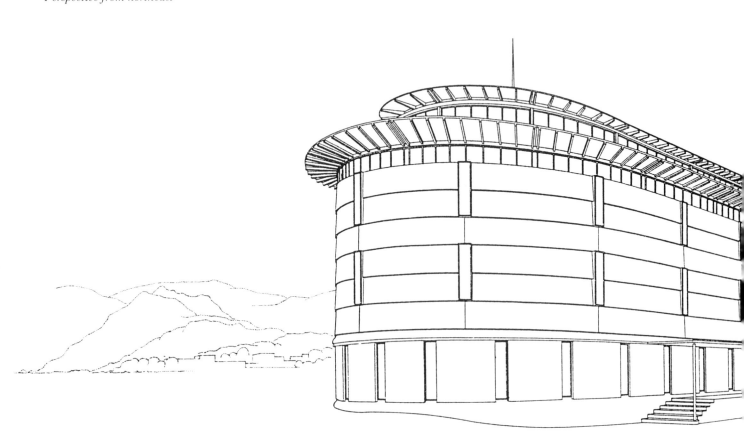

Site plan

BORIS PODRECCA

Mazda Lietz Showroom and Service Center ▪ Waidhofen, Lower Austria ▪ 1992

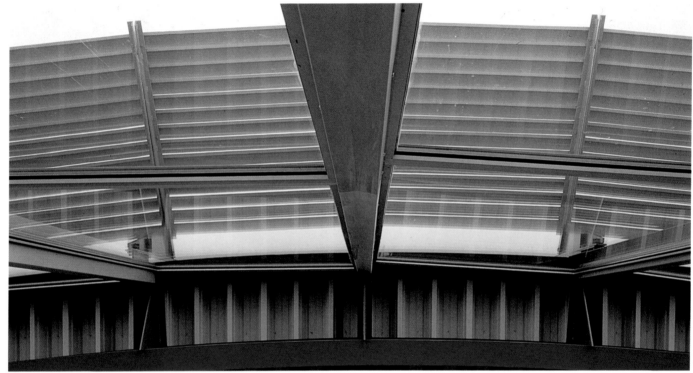

Podrecca connected this project to the surrounding landscape of the light-industrial perimeter of the city through the careful application of materials and disposition of structural elements. The project features three functional and physical sections: the automobile showroom, the service and repair area, and exterior components.

The quarter-circle of the showroom is enclosed by a two-story glass facade. A projecting steel roof and loggia mark the entrance. New cars are not Podrecca's only concern; the front facade also features a vehicle entrance into the repair area. Behind the entrance the infrastructure of the dealership becomes apparent: discussion areas, rest rooms, and a relaxation room. At this junction is an interior stair leading to offices on the level above.

The service area is housed in a square building constructed of reinforced concrete framed in steel. The facade is clad in metal panels with small protruding elements. The storage area for the large inventory of parts continues through two floors, well-lit by skylights. These spaces are adaptable and feature effective cross ventilation. On the north side is a large service loggia with a facade constructed of metal screens and movable doors.

The exterior components consist of three areas, for new cars, customer parking, and used cars. The mystery of how cars enter the showroom becomes an event: an earthen berm connects the outer bounds of the site to the built complex, evolving from a wall into a concrete display ramp that flows through the showroom following the curve of the building envelope at the second-floor level. It comes to an abrupt end at the front facade, where a new vehicle is parked.

The ramp and its display car become an elegant three-dimensional sign, sparing the landscape the usual eyesore of unrestrained billboards. The ramp invites one to imagine driving along its surface into the nucleus of the structure. It also unifies the two parts of the complex while keeping each distinct.

Perspective from southwest

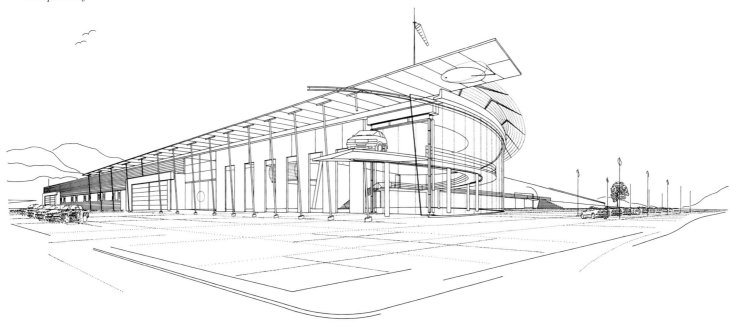

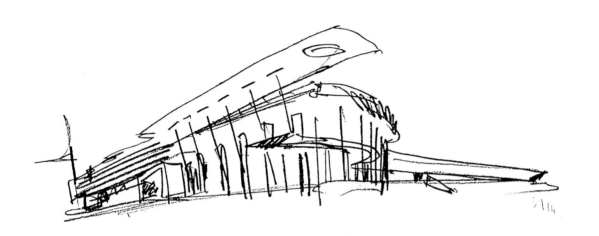

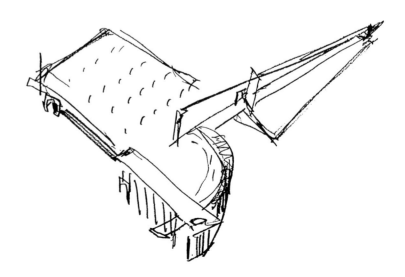

Roof plan

Site plan

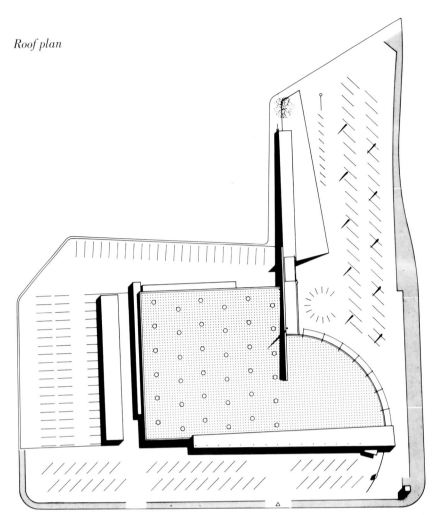

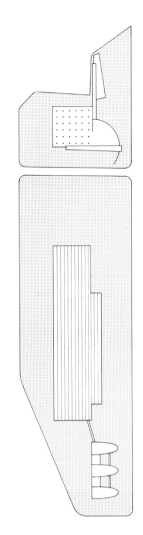

Ground floor plan

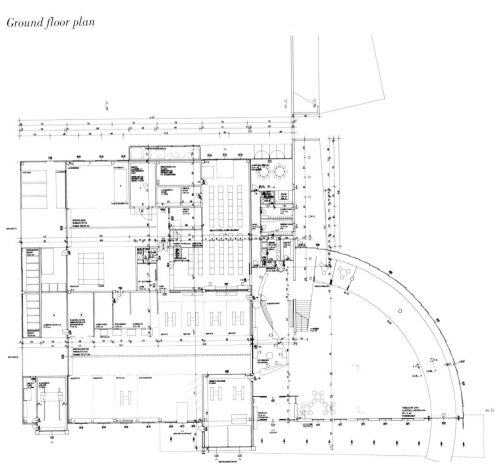

187

East elevation

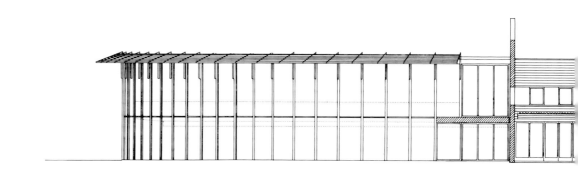

South elevation

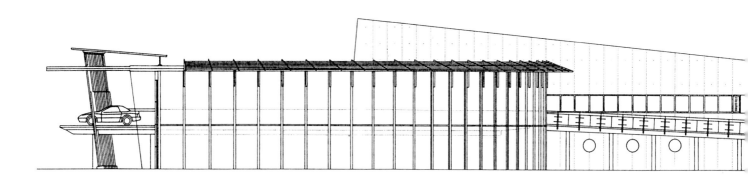

West elevation

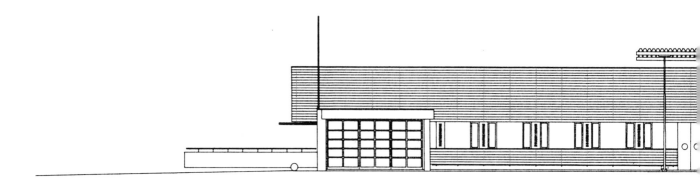

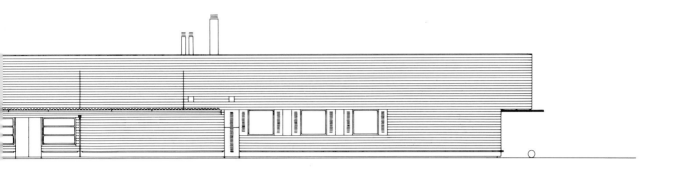

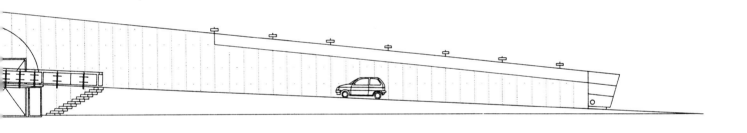

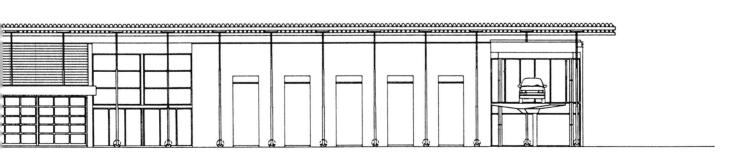

BORIS PODRECCA

Basler Insurance Company Headquarters ▪ *Vienna* ▪ *1993*

Podrecca's mixed-use office and retail space for the Basler Insurance Company in the Brigittenauer Lände area of Vienna responds to the urban context in several ways. Vienna's twentieth district is dominated by simple and repetitive tenements. A principle element in this rather dense part of the city is the Danube Canal, which offers spatial relief and the standard recreational activities of promenades, docks, and open spaces. Due to the large scale of this site, the building facade could respond to the equally extensive waterfront. Recent development at Othmargasse offered the opportunity to extend the complex and unite it with Brigittaplatz.

The design of this building addresses the larger context of the city block pattern while responding at a smaller scale to its specific location. Thus each of the three public facades is different, articulated in response to its orientation to the city. The elevation along Treustrasse features the traditional perforated wall. Toward Hirschvogelgasse, long bands of windows and parapets run along a curtain wall in front of a row of columns.

The project's most elaborate facade facing Brigittenauer Lände deviates from the otherwise strict adherence to the form of adjoining blocks. Its rounded curve at the right edge of the complex swells out and continues in long horizontal bands. These bands are composed of stacked sections of glazing and a regular grid of windows all the way to the corner of Hirschvogelgasse. Here a perforated wall slab faced with black granite rotates out of the general alignment, emphasizing the head of the entire complex. Its massing is expressionist yet simple, creating a distinct place while assuming its role in the urban fabric.

Ground floor plan

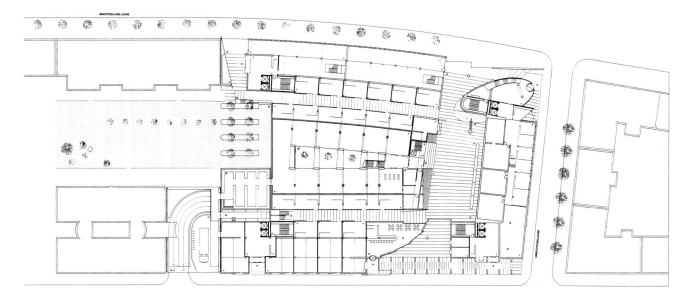

Brigittenauer Lände elevation

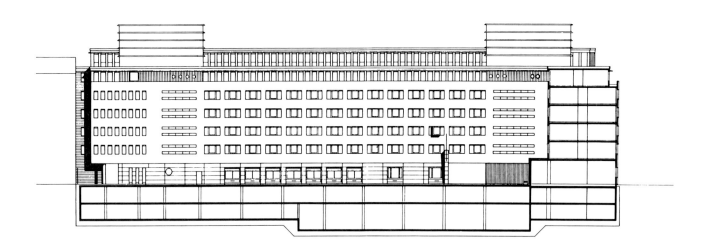

Treustrasse elevation

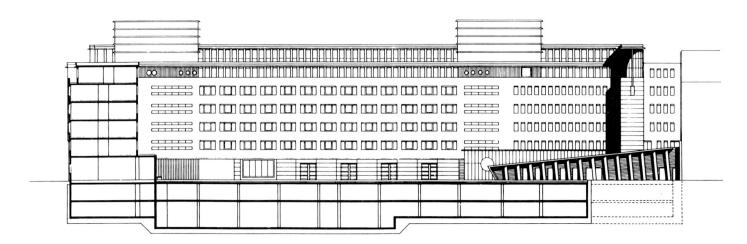

ANTON SCHWEIGHOFER

Competition Entry for the State Capital ▪ St. Pölten, Lower Austria ▪ 1989

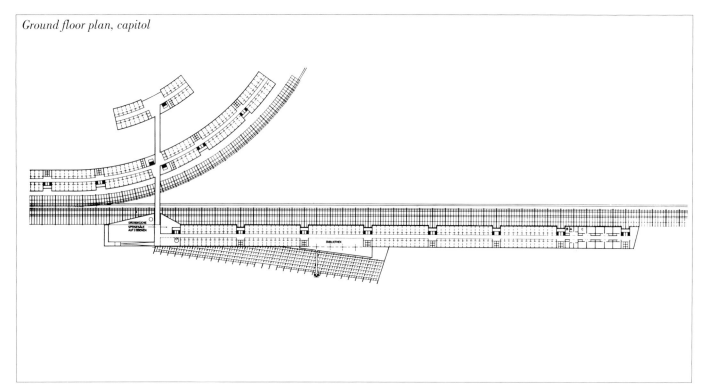

Ground floor plan, capitol

Schweighofer's competition entry for a new state capital deals with issues common to all large-scale urban interventions. Determining existing conditions in urban design and architecture requires addressing intimately all aspects of the problem, not just building pragmatically. Urban design and development are often constrained by the public's nostalgia for preservation, romantic hopes, the progressive desire for renewal, and political reality. A monumental solution for a specific public area (governmental, cultural, residential, commercial, or recreational) contradicts contemporary notions of the environment and democracy.

This proposal emphasizes that the historical urban fabric of this small town should continue to grow naturally without hostile interruption. To achieve this, direct and easily accessible paths from the main traffic artery to the government quarter and particularly to the new capitol are necessary. Further, the neglected railway area must be rejuvenated, the existing green space must be maintained, and property suited for residential purposes must not be wasted on office buildings. Even though the railway area is not the most popular site for the new government building, it is the most appropriate. Schweighofer's proposal integrates the new capitol into the main railway building, ensuring that it is functionally and visually accessible.

Perspective from south

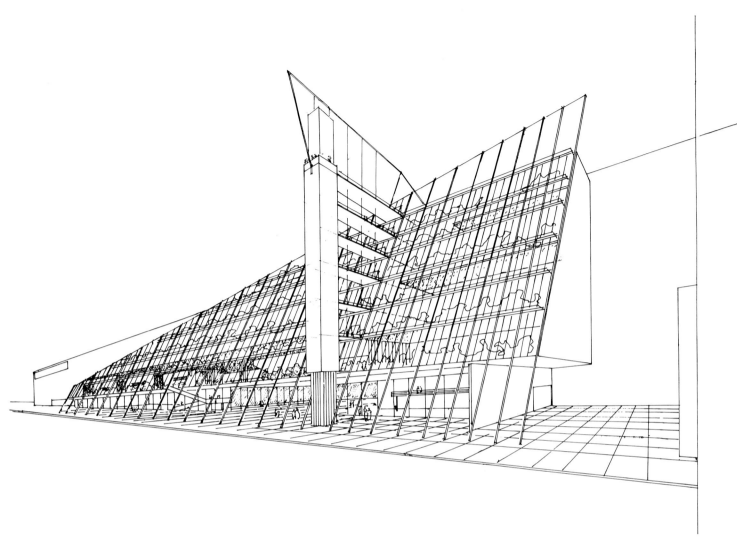

Site plan

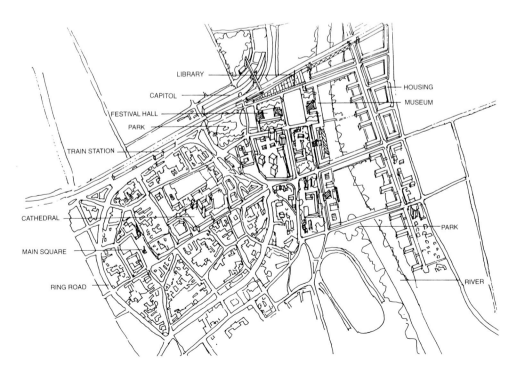

LIBRARY

CAPITOL

FESTIVAL HALL

PARK

TRAIN STATION

HOUSING

MUSEUM

CATHEDRAL

PARK

MAIN SQUARE

RING ROAD

RIVER

ANTON SCHWEIGHOFER

Stadtvillen Housing Complex, Gatterburggasse 2c ▪ Vienna ▪ 1989

The design of these two urban villas and kindergarten transforms a centralized floor plan to relate to the overall complex and site amenities. Thus, communal areas such as the courtyard, garden, and open walkways are incorporated into the buildings, enhancing the quality of apartment and city life. Spatial sequences, transitional spaces between private and public areas, and exterior and interior volumes encourage social interaction among residents. The restrained materials and absence of color give the buildings an elegant, classical presence in keeping with Viennese tradition.

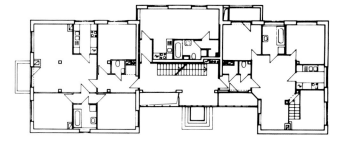

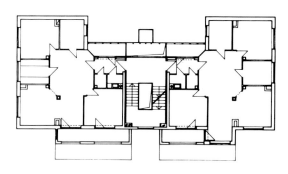

Ground floor plans

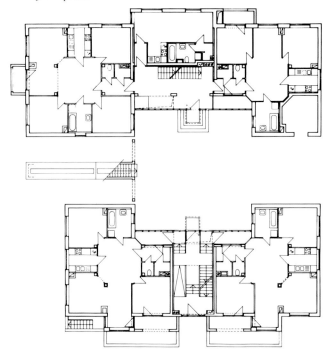

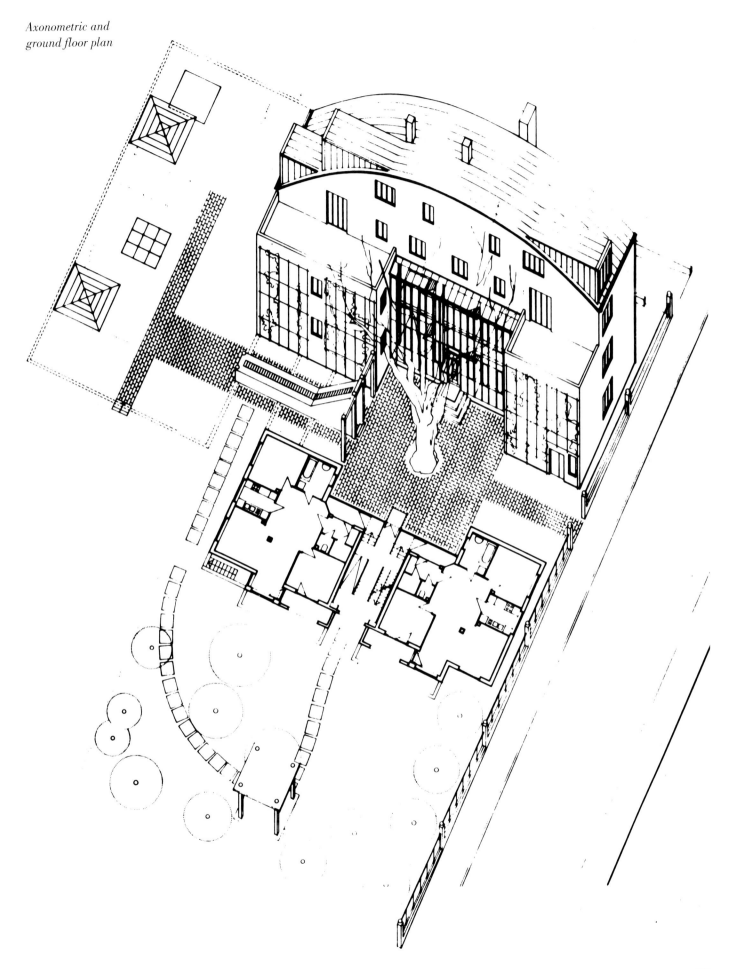

*Axonometric and
ground floor plan*

ANTON SCHWEIGHOFER

City Hall ▪ Mistelbach, Lower Austria ▪ 1989

Anton Schweighofer creates rationalist architecture in the modernist tradition. The Mistelbach City Hall, on the outskirts of Vienna, embodies formal and functional objectives generated from a distinct matrix of social responsibilities.

Schweighofer integrated a surrounding public park into the project as both an element of open space and a site for specific events. He envisioned a "garden temple" there for use as a cultural center by the local community. A small, classical existing building was converted into a restaurant and became an important element in planning the new building. The more formal elevation to the street defines the relationship to the existing urban fabric while using facade elements as communication tools to advertise current programs. This complex building is a vital, dynamic part of the town's civic activities, balancing informality and institutional rigor.

Perspective of main entrance from garden

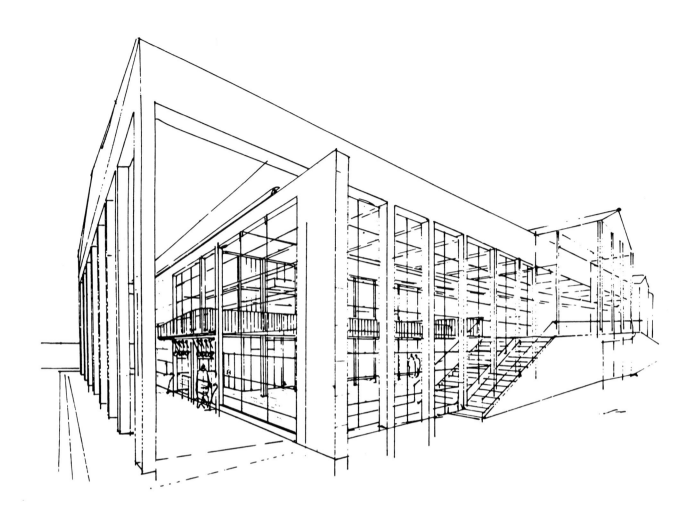

Basement level plan   *Entry level plan*   *Main level plan*

Exposed interior view from east

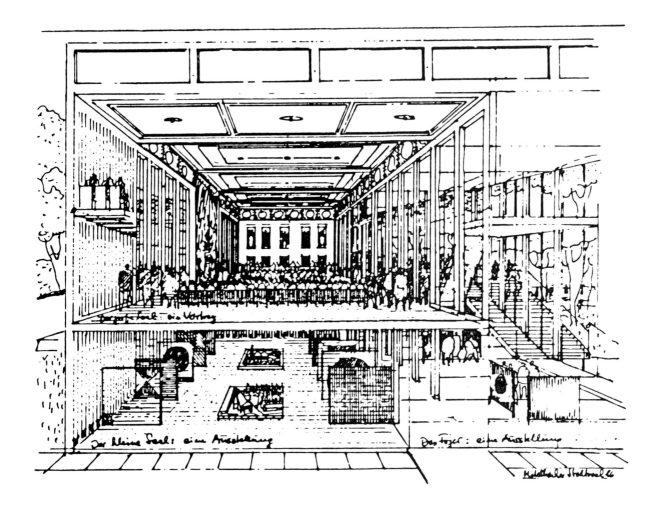

Cross section

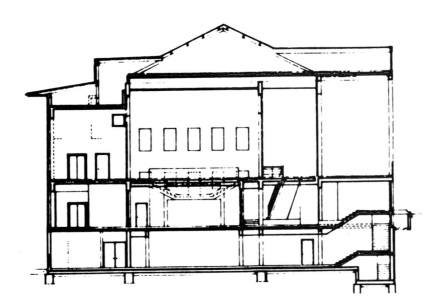

SZYSZKOWITZ-KOWALSKI

Harmisch House ▪ Burgenland ▪ 1988

A hunting lodge belonging to the same family that commissioned this project originally stood on this site. The client's substantial demands were rooted not so much in luxury as in the interpretation of a particular life-style and context. A certain grandeur and uniqueness was desired and delivered.

The building emphasizes exposure in two directions. The more public elements such as the access road, entrance, and office face north toward a valley and Kohfidisch, a neighboring village, commanding some of the best views. Above is a central hall with a cool north balcony protected from the sun.

In the opposite direction to the south, toward the Kaiserwald hills, are the living spaces. They consist of the southern part of the hall, the dining room and kitchen, and the living room, which extends to the outside as a walled-in courtyard. On the upper level, the two-story hall of the living area, accentuated by a large skylight, surrounds the library. From this gallery one reaches the five bedrooms and their baths.

Exploded floor plans

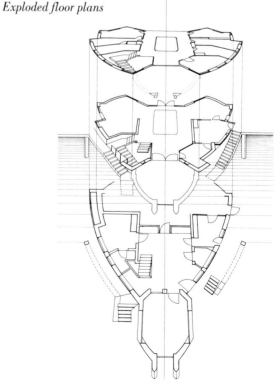

SZYSZKOWITZ-KOWALSKI

Institute for Biochemistry and Biotechnology, Technical University of Graz ▪ 1991

Michael Szyszkowitz and Karla Kowalski's competition-winning project uses its location at an intersection and the rectilinear public square (the Felix-Dahn-Platz) to direct attention to the public realm. The U-shaped building creates a termination point for a public axis that runs roughly north-south and passes through the building. This axis unifies the highly articulated building and the residual spaces between it and Schörgelgassse to the north, Mandelstrasse to the west, and Petergasse to the east. The building faces a children's playground to the northeast. The rest of the complex faces the chemical institute to the southwest and a park to the southeast. The square is bordered by mature trees and residential buildings.

Although complex and apparently capricious, the building's underlying plan, construction, and materials choices respond to the best traditions of modern architecture. This is evident in the floor plans of major spaces and support functions; the sections maximize the usable volume allowed by zoning restrictions.

The expressive formal language matches this building's program, which encourages discovery and surprise guided by logic and purpose.

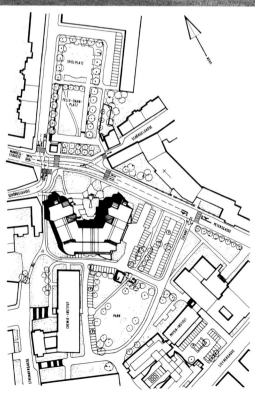

Ground floor plan

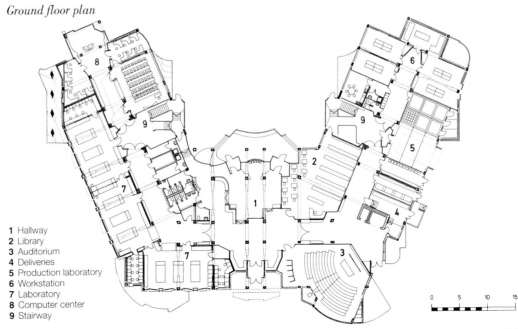

1 Hallway
2 Library
3 Auditorium
4 Deliveries
5 Production laboratory
6 Workstation
7 Laboratory
8 Computer center
9 Stairway

0   5   10   15

HEINZ TESAR

Schömer Headquarters ▪ Klosterneuberg, Lower Austria ▪ 1987

In his approach to this office space for a trading company Heinz Tesar relies on a traditional view of the office building while integrating work spaces and communal areas. The Schömer building does not typify office space on either exterior or interior. The immediately comprehensible design features a generous, well-lit multistory hall extending the full height of the building. The hall is the structure's central communal room, from which all offices are accessible. Vertical circulation, in the form of skeletal staircases, becomes the functional and artistic focal point of this space.

The building is set back from the street on a thirty-five centimeter-high earthen embankment. Reinforced concrete construction allows the greatest flexibility in office divisions. The exterior is stucco, differentiated by a spoon pattern on the lower level.

A protruding section, both concave and convex and covered by a separate roof, articulates the entrance. Roof terraces over the main building mass provide outdoor relaxation areas.

Ground floor plan

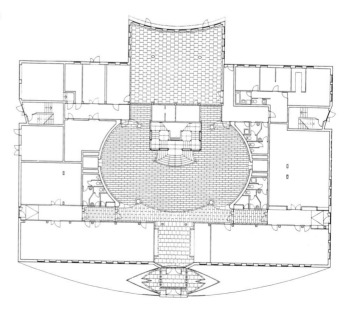

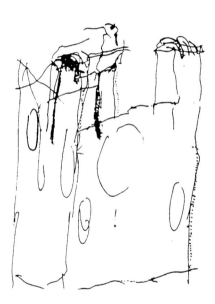

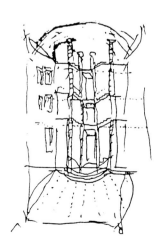

HEINZ TESAR

Rooftop Apartment, Hauptplatz 17 ▪ Linz ▪ 1990

Tesar redefines the house type in this rooftop apartment in Linz. The professional musicians who commissioned the project inspired the design: Tesar used the long shape of the existing structure metaphorically, to suggest a violin. The central atrium represents the instrument's sound holes, the kitchen and terrace are the curves of its body, the long axial skylight represents the strings, and the gently curving roof exaggerates the curvature of the violin's upper body.

If the violin was the departure point, other concepts soon came into play. The long band of skylights accentuates the axiality of the existing structure. The small circular atrium, with a simple glass skylight, separates the first and second thirds of the apartment. Around this atrium cluster the living room, hall, kitchen, and studio. Between the second and final thirds of the apartment, another skylight runs perpendicular to the main axis and bisects the long skylight, shedding light on the hall and studio.

Toward the front of the building, facing the main square, is a terrace with a pergola. The entrance to the apartment is one level below, accessible via an existing stair. Simple materials finish the interior, with plaster walls, wood floors, and a special stone floor for the atrium.

Axonometric

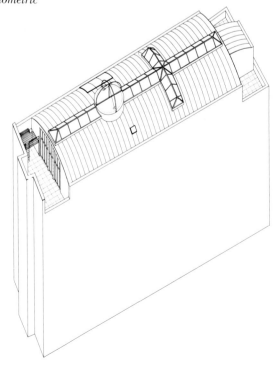

Facade showing rooftop atrium

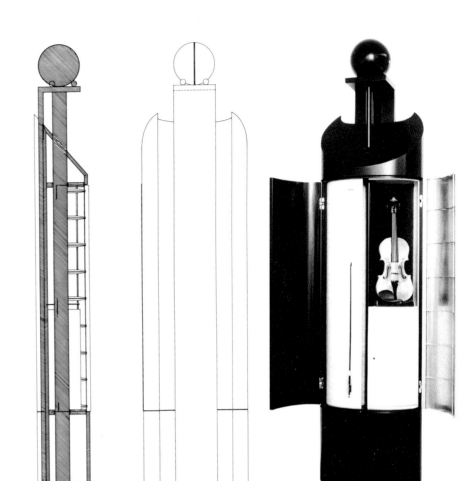

Floor plan

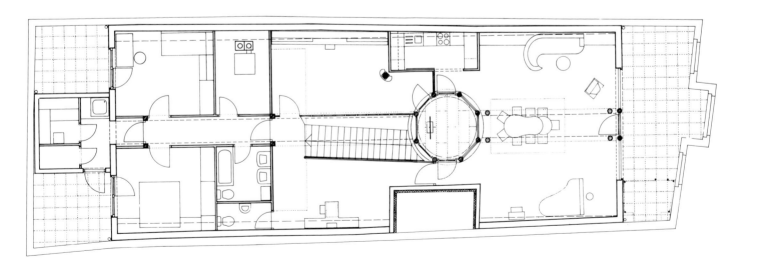